Cont

Introduction

...

Introduction

In this book, I hope you will find everything you need to know in order to set up a successful craft business from home, using Etsy, your own website or selling in person. Despite the huge range of craft products available to sell, you will be able to apply most of the principles from this book to the craft of your choice.

I have divided this book into small, bite-sized sections so that you don't have to spend hours reading unnecessarily. Time is precious to everyone and I am sure you'll appreciate being able to dip in and out at your leisure. I want you to get the most of out of this book, no matter how little spare time you have.

At the end of each chapter, I have included both a workbook page and two case studies to aid you in developing your business. As a former teacher, it was drummed into me that learning doesn't just happen in the classroom. That's why I've added questions for you to reflect on what you have learnt, in order for you to get the most out of this experience. The inclusion of case studies allows you to see how two different businesses may implement what is discussed in the chapter.

Before you start reading, I would strongly recommend using either a digital or paper 'Brain Dump' system. You might use it to complete the workbook pages included in this book or simply to have somewhere to think of and record ideas. I tend to use a mixture of both; a cheap notebook that stays on my desk and Microsoft One Note for my virtual Brain Dumping. I always find I have the best ideas when I am least expecting them so being able to dump them until I am able to think about them in more depth is really handy for me.

You can either work through the book from start to finish or engage as you feel you need to. Bear in mind, however, that the workbook exercises build on each other so if you miss a chapter or read them out of order, they might not make as much sense.

The workbook questions are designed to get you to think about the topics in each of the lessons. It is up to you how you want to respond to the questions. You don't have to answer the questions fully; if you can only think of one reason to do something, that's fine. I've included more options in order to get you to think. I suggest having a dedicated notebook or folder where you can write your answers to the questions in order to get the most out of this book.

PART I

Getting Ready to Start Your Business

Why do You Want to Start a Business?

Before we explore potential ideas and the planning stages of a business, I feel it's important to establish why you want to start a business. I was one of those people who always had 100 ideas for businesses and unsurprisingly, I didn't do any of them. Why? Because each idea wasn't focused on what I hoped to gain from running a business. Being a virtual assistant, for example, would bring in money, which was a big motivation, but I'd also be working every weekend so I would miss out on family time, which is a key motivating factor for me. Being someone else's assistant also didn't inspire huge levels of enthusiasm or passion.

I like organising and setting up systems but doing it for someone else on a sunny Sunday morning was never going to spark my creative juices. That's why I looked at making jewellery. I'd always liked making things and as I am passionate about my products It was also something I could continue to do when my daughter was born. I now work mostly when she's napping in the day or when she's in bed.

. . .

Some Reasons You May Want to Start a Business Could Include:

- Money: Let's not beat around the bush, we all need It and there is no shame in admitting that it is a key motivator to setting up your own business.
- Time: Are you great in the morning? Do you have a child who doesn't quite know when to nap? Working for yourself gives you the ability to choose how much time you will devote to something and when. No more nine to five, so you can still pick the kids up after school.
- Flexibility: Your daughter is sick? Your son has a sports day coming up? If you have an understanding manager, you might be able to take time off. Not all managers are quite as sympathetic. When you are your own boss, you decide when you take time off and when you work. You even get the perk of deciding when you feel you need a pay rise. Not many jobs give you that choice.
- Boredom: In my naivety as a first-time mum, I honestly thought I'd - wait for it- get bored! While changing nappies can get dull, I don't think it is possible to get 'bored' with a young child. I don't have the time. I do however feel that my mind needs stretching and putting time into a business I am passionate about really gives me something to remind myself that while I might be a mum, but I am still me too.
- Passion and skill: Do you have a skill that you like doing and are good at? Maybe you are great at making soaps or handmade dog treats?

Being passionate and good at something is a huge part of making a business successful.

- To help people: Maybe you have an idea that can provide great pleasure or even help people. One example of this is knitted octopuses for premature babies. While there are charities who provide them for free, supplies are limited, so similar types of products are available to buy.

Pros and Cons of Starting a Business

There is no getting away from the fact that starting a business can be both rewarding and challenging. That's why it's so important to go in with your eyes wide open.

Pros of Running a Business:

- You can structure your days as you want.
- You can build a business you are passionate about.
- Your earning potential is decided by you.
- Being in control and your own boss.
- Being at home if you have children/commitments.

Cons of Running a Business:

- Mundane tasks you don't like doing still have to be done.

- There can be financial risk and income is not guaranteed.
- You may have to work around the children's holidays.
- You may struggle to switch off and so work long hours.
- Working from home can mean more distractions.

As with anything in life, you will have to compromise. It might mean working when the children have gone to bed and skipping the latest TV drama. The payoff is that you can take time off in the day as and when you need to (even if it's just to catch up on chores so you have your weekend free). You can overcome most 'Cons' if you are creative.

3

How Much do You Realistically
Need to Earn?

I didn't design this book to be one which suggested you will earn a '*Six Figure Salary in 14 Days with No Work Involved*'. They always seem a little too good to be true! Pretty much everyone would like a six-figure salary and there is nothing stopping you from pushing for one with your business, it's a great goal to aim for. But if we are being realistic, it will take a lot of hard work, time and resources to do this, not something you can achieve in the short term.

Having extra money, even a few hundred pounds, can still make a positive impact on your finances. It's a holiday, it's taking the kids out on the weekend, it's going out for food a few times a month. If you have a working partner, you may not need to go back to work if you want to stay with your children until you are happy to leave them. You might be on maternity and not qualify for financial help. You are the type of person I wrote this book for.

When I sat down and worked out a budget, I realised I didn't need that much extra a month to make a huge difference to my lifestyle. As a minimum I wanted to cover my own personal bills (about £300 per month at the time) so I felt like I was making a valued contribution. Anything extra was a bonus. I like being able to help out financially but also be able to spend time with my daughter. Some months (Christmas for example), I can make two/three times my normal monthly amount. I do work weekends around Christmas to keep up with demand but as I do it when my daughter is sleeping, she doesn't miss out on my time.

I know as my daughter gets older, I'll have more time to spend on my business and therefore can generate more money. But for now, I have a happy balance; I am able to work around nap times and significant events with little disruption to family life.

Before starting a business, I'd strongly recommend sitting down and working out how much you'd like to earn and examine if there are ways to cut costs at home, so that if circumstances dictated you could afford to earn less.

How Will You Fund Your Business?

Even if you have a rough idea of what you want to sell, funding the initial stock or materials needed to set up may not have crossed your mind at this stage.

Despite what some business gurus say, you don't need a huge amount of money to set up. Lots of successful small businesses start as a side hustle, with minimal start-up funds and expand as they become more successful.

Setting up my jewellery business required very little in the way of start-up costs. A website, stock and a better printer all came in at under £200. If you decide to sell on other platforms, such as Etsy, they'll take their fees once you've sold the item, so you don't have to pay to start trading.

Having done a personal budget, it's time to do a business budget. You'll need to think what you realistically need to start selling today. There is a blank template in the work book.

My Initial Budget Looked Like This:

- Paper stickers: £12.87
- Printer: £45
- Ink: £7.99
- Chains: £21.99
- Ring hoops: £ 3.65
- Large gems: £9.97
- Small gems: £4.45
- Backs: £ 5.97
- Glue: £6.99
- Envelopes: £8.75
- Bubbles wrap £10.99
- Cardboard boxes: £6.99
- Labels: £2.98
- Website hosting: £15p/m
- Website domain: £4.35
- WordPress theme: £30

Total: £197.94

Things like a theme and printer will be one off costs, but if you don't need·and can manage without them for while it will cost you even less. As jewellery is delicate, I have to spend a larger amount on packaging than someone who knits for example.

While I had a larger outlay than some start-ups, I was able to sell each necklace for £13.95 making a total sale (for 20) of £279. It's not a huge amount of profit to start with, but once I was able to order in larger quantities (and not regularly having to make less cost effective one off purchases), I was able to keep more and more of the profit.

One thing I would suggest is to have a 'Trial and Error'

fund. As with all craft, having to try out new ideas can cost a lot of wasted materials. As a hobbyist, that's not such a problem, as a business, it can be. So, set aside a small budget to allow you to expand your range.

If you don't think you can self-fund, there are other ways to gain funding:

- Bank loans/credit card: You will need to produce a business plan to show you could make a profit. If you need something big for your business, then this can be a good option. Just make sure you can make the repayments.
- Kickstarter: you'll need to be willing to give discounts or extras to gain followers. People will want to see what their money is paying for so be prepared to explain what you are spending other people's money on.
- Family and friends: depending on how supportive the people you know are, borrowing can be helpful and little to no interest will be applied. Just make sure to pay back on time as you don't want to fall out with anyone.
- Grants: There are charities such as The Princes Trust who offer funding for start-ups. The government also offers a New Enterprise Allowance if you are on certain benefits. Again, you will need to produce a business plan, but you are also given a mentor to help you.

Be aware when using external funding sources as you may

have to provide some guarantee (as with a loan) that you'll pay it back. You will also be expected to explain decisions you want to make. If you can save some money and keep your costs down to the bare minimum, you may not need any external funding at all.

Common Business Mistakes

- Not Planning: You wouldn't go into an exam unprepared, so why would you start a business like that? Get the groundwork completed and the rest will be a lot easier.
- Spending Too Much: Start with the bare minimum. Once you have made a profit, then expand. Even large companies do that. The founder of Amazon started in his garage, not a warehouse.
- No Passion: Not choosing a business that you are passionate about will mean you are likely to fail. As you will be doing 99% of the work, it's important to actually enjoy what you are doing.
- Not Conducting Market Research: Crafts can be an over saturated market, so you need to make sure you stand out. Researching your competition and seeing how you can do it better than them will help you home in the ideal customers for your business.
- No Ideal Customers: Through your market research, you'll find your ideal customer. Any

new decisions should be based on these customers and whether it will encourage them to buy from you.

- Over/ Under-Pricing Goods: The simple reality is that you make money from your product. Don't be scared of overcharging, you can decide its worth. On the same token, don't overcharge unless your item is greatly superior in quality than other people's products. Don't rip people off- they'll just not buy from you.
- Trying to Be Perfect: One of the reasons people like handmade items is because they are unique. Even if you make 100 candles, they'll all be slightly different and special. You should obviously make things to the best of your ability, as well as running your business well. We all make mistakes, trying something and making a mistake is better than never trying it at all.

How do You Find Support for Your Business?

While this book aims to cover most of what you'll need to set up a business, you might feel you need more support on your area of expertise.

Facebook Groups

Hands down my favourite type of support because there are groups for everything. Selling candles? There's a group for that. Making bespoke jewellery? There's a group for that too. I have complied a list of groups in the back of this book to help you find one to support your niche.

These groups work best when there is some give and take. Even if you are just starting out, you could give feedback. It might be a discount code to a supplier or advising someone on your experiences with a hosting company. Everyone wants to help each other.

I would aim to join a few specific groups that are niche and then some more general small business groups to help you with the practical elements, such as websites.

· · ·

Local Councils

The support varies from council to council. Most will have some sort of business support. They might offer:

- Hot desk work spaces.
- A course on running a business.
- Funding for start ups.
- Advice sessions.
- Help with business planning .
- A business advisor.
- Practical contacts.
- Test areas i.e. spaces in markets.

If you check out your local council webpage under 'Employment' or 'Business Advice', you should be able to find out what is being offered. Another option is to find out how to contact your local chamber of commerce. This is a local business network to provide contacts, trading help and ways to test products.

Regional Business Support

These are regional rather than local and will help people who live in specific areas. They usually offer training and support as well as offering affordable office space. Your local council may list regional office on the council website. Alternatively, type into a search engine "business support for" and your location.

Growth Hubs

There are 38 across England which offer local and national business support. They will also put you in contact with mentors who can help your set up your business. In addition, they also offer general advice.

The Princes Trust Enterprise Programme

The Princes Trust programme offers great information for business start-ups. Their introductory 'Business Plan Pack' is particularly helpful when first starting out on developing a business.

Direct Gov

Good for information on legal matters such as tax or employment questions. If you are not in the UK, then check out your country's official government website as most will likely offer legal and employment advice.

Workbook: Part One

Lesson One

- Why do you want to start a business? Try to think of three reasons why you want to start a business.
- Why have you chosen these reasons? Write a short sentence explaining your reasoning for the choice of each.
- Example: *Time- I want to spend more time with my family.*

Lesson Two

- Draw two columns, label one 'Pros' and the second 'Cons', now think of five facts to place in each column. You can be as vague or specific as you like.
- Example:

- *Pros: I can be my own boss.*
- *Cons: Having an unreliable income.*

Lesson Three

- Writing a budget might not be the most appealing aspect of running a business but it is important to see where you could cut costs. The more you save, the less you need to earn. Add or remove what you need to personalise the example budget below. Make sure you check comparison websites to see if you can get a better deal.

- **Income**

- Housing
- Mobiles
- Internet/home phone/tv package
- Tv license
- Water
- Council tax
- Gas/ electricity
- Car insurance/tax
- Transport costs (Including petrol)

- **Outgoings**

- Home Insurance:
- Medical insurance:

- Food shopping
- Eating out
- Children's school costs (uniform, fees, lunches, stationary, trips etc):
- Adult Clothes:
- Children clothes:
- Toiletries:
- Medical costs (including dentist):
- Pet insurance:
- Pet medical costs:
- Pet food

- After studying your budget, suggest three things could you do to save money?
- Example: *I would see if I could reduce eating out to twice a month as opposed to three. This would save an extra £30 a month.*

Lesson Four

- What essential items would you need to buy for your business to be able to start making and selling immediately? You can include a website if you think it is essential.
- What other items would you like to buy for your business?
- For the items you need, research the costs of each item. How much will it cost you to start up?
- Think of three places you could apply to gain a grant or loan for your business. What are the pros and cons for each of these options?

- Example: *I could get a loan from my parents. The pros would be that I wouldn't be charged interest and I could pay it back slowly. The cons would be that it could put a strain on our relationship if I didn't pay quickly or if something went wrong, as their money isn't protected.*

Lesson Five

- Can you think of three mistakes someone might make when starting a new business?
- Which is the most worrying mistake you feel you might make when starting your business?
- How could you overcome this?
- Example: *I initially spent too much when setting up my business on things I didn't need. The way I would recommend overcoming this is thinking about what I would need for my business if I had to set up tomorrow. I would limit what I bought that way.*

Lesson Six

Facebook Groups

- Using the list provided, or by completing your own research, join three Facebook groups in your niche. What are the names of the groups you have joined?
- Using the list provided, or by completing your own research, find and join three non-niche groups. What are the names of the groups you have joined?
- Choose one niche group and one non-niche group. Think of a question you would like to

ask in each type of group. What are your two
questions?

- To make sure you are also giving back to the
groups you have joined, find three questions in
either a niche or non-niche group and answer
them. What questions did you choose and how
did you answer them?

- Example: *If someone had asked for advice on logos for
their new business, I might give my opinion on the one I
liked most and why.*

Local Councils

- Go on to your local councils' Business Support
page. What support do their offer?
- Which offerings do you think would be of the
most use to you? Why?
- Choosing one of the offerings above, what
could you do today that would allow you to
make use of that resource?
- Example: *I might write a letter to enquire about a
mentoring programme.*

Regional Business Support

- What regional business support is available to
you in your area?
- Which offerings do you think would be the
most helpful to you?
- Choosing one of the offerings above, what

could you do today that would allow you to make use of that resource?

- Example: *I shall book myself in for a business support meeting to get advice on financing a new business.*

Growth Hubs

- Does your area offer local growth hubs? If not, do they run something similar?
- Which services does it run that you feel would be of benefit to you?

The Princes Trust

- Have a look at The Princes Trust Website. Choose four resources that you think would help you set up a business. Which four things did you choose?

Direct Gov

- The Direct Gov website is helpful for finding information about self-employment and tax. Can you find two other topics on the website that would help you in your business?

End of Chapter Questions

- Which three parts of this chapter have been the most helpful to you?
- Choose one thing from this chapter that you could use and implement today. What have you chosen and how are you going to implement it?

PART II

Ideas

8

Brain Storming Ideas

Thinking of a business idea can be daunting, especially if you've never run a business before. I've tried to break everything down into bite sized chunks in order for you to really focus on what it is you are passionate enough about to make money from.

You might want to grab a pen and paper for this exercise.

For this first part, let's start with you. What are your skills? Are you good at selling, writing or even cooking? These skills don't have to be work related but just what you think you're good at.

Secondly, what are your hobbies? It could be creative writing, sewing or music for example. These are things you like doing.

. . .

For the third and final question, are you concerned about passive income? You might not be the world's best knitter, but you might be great at making knitting patterns. Passive income is about making something once and selling it multiple times.

If I was to do this exercise myself, I would summarise as follows:

- Skills: organising, solving problems, writing and cooking
- Hobbies: reading, jewellery making, knitting and creative writing

Yes, definitely something to consider (for example once this book is printed it will require no further work from me but hopefully will earn me some money).

With List one, I may struggle to make something I could sell on Etsy or on a website, however, if I am a good cook, I should be able to follow recipes. Accordingly, beauty products as well as soap and candles might be something I could do. With my second list, I could choose jewellery or knitting. I am far better (and enjoy it more) at making jewellery than knitting, so this could be a good choice.

With my final point, if I was to choose something like jewellery or candles, I could sell "how to" guides or courses to supplement the income from my product sales.

After completing the above exercise, you might have at least one idea for a business. If you don't, no need to panic. Personally, I have had some of my best ideas after mulling things over. The showers is always my go-to place to think of ideas. Having a pen and paper by your bed at night enables you to jot down any ideas while they are fresh in your memory. If you are struggling, take a day or two to think about what you would like to do or what you are good at. Keep a page in a notebook or in your note-taking app and drop in any ideas you have until you have at least five. Transfer it to a spider diagram if it makes it easier for you to take notes.

Ideas:

- Sewing
- Jewellery
- Soap making
- Candles
- Knitting

Now is the time to think how you can be different- your unique selling point.

You don't have to reinvent the wheel, but it may help to be more niche. You'll need to do this in order to find your ideal customer. When I did this, I spent a few days just jotting down ideas and produced something like this.

Ideas (Expanded):
Sewing:

- Kids clothing
- Kids toys
- Bags for equipment

Jewellery:

- Silver
- Letter stamping
- Cosplay

Soap Making:

- Weird combinations
- Organic/natural
- Unusual shapes

Candles:

- Organic/natural
- Vegan
- Essential oils

Knitting:

- Blankets
- Banners
- Toys

I had set myself a target of three for each idea, but you can add more or less. The next stage is to narrow down your idea.

Passion: Does any idea seem a bore or something you would dread doing. If this is the case, remove it from the list. Life is too short. I completely removed sewing as I wasn't passionate about it.

Do I Have the Skills to Do It Professionally? There is nothing wrong with learning the skills, but you want to set up a business now, you'll need to find something you are passionate about and have the skills to do. I removed knitting and soap making as I wasn't that skilled in soap making and I wasn't passionate enough about it to learn. I like knitting as a hobby, but I am limited in my skills

Is It Currently Realistic? Do you have space for larger crafts or to let them dry/cure from children or pets? Do you have the money to buy expensive equipment? I love making candles but with an infant and a nosy dog, I wouldn't have space to cure things away from little hands or paws. It would also require me to spend a decent amount on set up costs which I couldn't afford.

Is It Marketable? Is the market over saturated? This stage requires some research. You should now have one main category (e.g. jewellery) with a few subheadings. Using your subheadings, go on to Etsy and find how many people are selling those things.

- Silver: 4,288,641
- Letter stamping: 110,293
- Specific Cosplay: 210

You don't just have to use Etsy, but it gives a good idea of an item's popularity. So, for me, it was a very simple choice, 210 vs 4,288,641 people to compete with. It's still a lot but I can work on my USP. If you aren't able to narrow down enough, think how easy you could be unique. Maybe you could use real gold or silver? You could source all materials from your country or even locally. Putting an eco-slant on your product would also make you stand out while helping to save the planet. Don't worry if it takes a while to find your project idea. It is best to wait and get a great idea that you are passionate about than one that makes you uninspired and so less dedicated.

9

Market Research

Before you can even start to make and sell a product, you'll need to conduct some market research. This doesn't mean you'll have to go and ask random people in the street what they think of your idea. Market research can be a lot less daunting.

Ways to Conduct Market Research:

Ask Groups on Facebook

Remember earlier when I said to join Facebook groups? Conducting market research in these groups can be really useful. If you are looking to see what is popular at the moment, then I would join hobby groups as you can browse and observe. If you want to ask a specific business question in a hobby group, make sure you ask the admins first.

. . .

Check Out Similar Products and Their Reviews

When I first started making necklaces, the first thing I did was check similar product reviews. I found the positive comments, such as how well made something was and then I looked at the negative reviews, which included things such as expensive shipping and items not being realistic. I knew I could attract customers if I made an item that was realistic, retailed cheaper and shipped quickly. I also made an effort to present my necklaces in velvet pouches or small boxes to keep them secure and look more attractive and higher end.

If you want to take this a step further and your funding allows, buy a few products similar to yours at different price points so you can see what your competition is doing. You might want to start high end but realise it would be a cost your ideal customers would not pay.

Searching Keywords on Etsy and Search Engines

This is a great way to see what other people are doing and find out trends. Brain storming several keywords to identify your products and see how you can make it more niche will help you find your ideal customers.

An example I might find if I searched for candles on google would be:

- Shaped candles
- Carved candles
- Eco candles
- Candles with items inside them
- Non-scented
- Beeswax candles
- Essential oil candles

There is no limit to the amount of words you can search for.

Trending Items

On Etsy, type in 'Trending now item' as a good way to find out what is selling really well in your category. You can also start typing the name of your item and see what Etsy suggests in the drop-down menu below. The search engine will show what customers have typed in when searching for items like yours.

Once you're in a category, look at the number of sales sellers have. You can take this a step further by looking at their reviews. You can't see how many of individual items the seller has sold but you can see how popular items are by how many people leave reviews on the item.

Pinterest and Instagram

These are good places to find out overall trends such as colours, themes or textures that are in favour at the moment. You can type your product in to the search engine and see what pictures are being shared/liked the most. You might be able to develop even more of a niche product this way.

Ideal Customer

When selling a product there are two ways to appeal:

Popular Market: It's the hottest trend right now and people are desperate for this product. To succeed, you'll need to be both different and the same; quicker shipping, better quality materials or cheaper products while meeting customer criteria.

Niche: Refine a popular item so it sits in a smaller group, scented candles is big business, but you are competing with a lot of rivals. Try natural scented (essential oils) with flower petals melted into them. They could be delicately scented which may make them more expensive, but this would appeal to certain people. It is better to be a leading player in a small market than get lost in a very large one.

Deciding which route to take will influence who you see as your ideal customer. Through your research, you would have met a lot of people, who like what you might make. It's your job to build a profile so that you give these people what they want. My example would be:

My Ideal Customer:

- Likes nice packaging.
- Likes the nostalgia factor.
- Is a woman aged 15-30.
- Will pay £10-£20.
- Wants fast shipping.
- Wants good quality materials but not high end.

I found all this out through my market research. I now know where to target adverts and concentrate my efforts. Trying to appeal to men who want to spend £5 isn't going to make me much money or be a good use of my time.

. . .

Unique Selling Point

Now you've done your research, it's time to think about your unique selling point. You need to think how you are going to be different from your competitor. An example would be:

- Price: I am going to be cheaper.
- Accuracy: I am going to make my product realistic.
- Shipping: I will ship within two days.

There will be benefits and costs to these. A cheaper price means either less profit or lower quality. So, I won't be using expensive backs for my necklaces (as high end isn't important to my customers), but I can compromise and use gold chains as these are higher quality and not that much more expensive. They are also a good selling point.

I need to be able to sum up what I hope to do in a few sentences. Using my USP's my summary would be:

I make replica necklaces from popular films. I use good quality materials, but I price affordably. I also aim to ship within two days.

Being able to summarise like this will keep you on the right track when designing products. If it doesn't fit into these sentences, then you need to go back to the drawing board. Specialise even further and write a tagline which will make it very easy for a customer to identify you and your brand.

Affordable, high quality replica necklaces with quick shipping.

Coming up with a great tagline will take some thought. It's worth spending time with some ideas you have and deciding which fits best with your USP.

10

Business Plan

You've now got your idea and done your research. Now what? This is where a business plan comes in. It takes all of your current knowledge and puts it into a document that will help you plan how you will move your business forward. Some of these categories can't be addressed now but you can make notes and return as you progress through the book.

Business plans can come in all shapes and sizes but to make it simple, I've used categories.

1. Three Sentences Summing Up My Idea

- This is to keep you aware of the overall purpose of your business. You experimented with this in the previous chapter and can use it here. You'll need to make sure you explain what you do and why you are different.

2. One Sentence On the Idea

- You did this in the last chapter too. It's your tagline and something you might later put on your logo or website.

3. Ideal Customer

- You can either use your bubble from the last chapter or lay it out in a different way. As you gather more information, you can add to your ideal customer profile.

4. Competition

- During your research, you came across a variety of businesses. Who do you think you would be competing against? Think about price, quality, similarity and how established they are. Use your USP section to see where they are competing with you.

5. USP

- This is where you analyse the competition and explain how you are different and could solve some of the complaints other businesses had.

6. Pricing and Costs

- This will be addressed later on in the book. In this area, you will write out your day to day running costs and also your pricing to cover this. If you have decided the range you are going to charge, place this here too with a justification to how you reached this decision.

7. Funding

- As mentioned in an earlier chapter, you will need to find a way to fund your business. You don't have to rely on just one place to find funding.

8. Where Are You Going to Sell?

- This will be covered in chapter four. You can either focus on just one place or use a mixture of sales methods. Some smaller products may do better online than in person, especially if they are niche.

9. Marketing

- In the last chapter, you conducted a large amount of market research, this will help you when you come to Chapter Five on marketing, where you can fill this area out. You'll want to include a brief strategy on why you think this will.

10. Set Up

- Lastly, how will you be setting up as a business? In chapter seven you will be given information to help you choose whether to be self-employed or register as a business and why you may want to choose that route.

Don't feel that you have to fill all this in on one day. The idea is to add to your knowledge, at your own pace, as you go along. It may be useful to jot notes down before you come to the relevant chapter.

11

Where Can I Get Stock?

Getting good quality stock at a reasonable price can make or break a business. You can have an item that sells in the thousands but that's no use to you if the materials to make it cost more than you can sell it for.

When it comes to stock, you need to break down everything you need into key areas. To get my jewellery to my customer I need the following:

- A Necklace: Chains, jump rings, backings, stickers, big green gems, small red gems, glue, wire crimpers.
- Packaging: Velvet bags, envelopes, bubble wrap, branded stickers, parcel boxes, tape, postage stickers and address labels.

It took a long time to research where to get all of my stock. It then took more time to see if I could get items cheaper.

As you expand, you may be able to get costs down by going to a supplier and ordering in bulk.

Once you have a list of what you need, it's time to go shopping. To rationalise your research try to be as specific as possible at first. Rather than type 'gold chains', try '18-inch gold plated chains' as that was what I wanted. If no results were displayed, I would take a step back by reducing the length of the search terms, for example you could remove the word 'plated'. You have to experiment with wordings to find exactly what you are looking for.

If you don't know what something is called, look at other sellers' listings. I remember researching the shape of a gem when I was first making my necklaces. In my head I knew what the shape was, but I didn't know its technical name. so, I googled 'cuts of diamonds' to see if the shape was one used in high end jewellery. I found they were called Navette or Marquise cuts. It saved hours of searching.

Places to Find Stock- Generic:

eBay

I get most of my stock from suppliers on eBay. I am able to negotiate with suppliers while also having the added protection of eBays refund policy should something go wrong. Some items are from the UK, others come internationally. There is a good range of products available at reasonable prices.

- What it's good for: Everything. Postal items can be extremely cheap.
- What it's not good for: If you need things in a hurry.

Amazon

Usually more expensive than eBay, but if you have Amazon Prime, you can get items using next day delivery.

- What it's good for: Rush items. Good selection of postage, materials and bigger items.
- What it's not good for: Cost and ranges of quality.

Etsy

A good place to find excess stock from sellers. If you make one-off pieces, you can find some unique materials here.

- What it's good for: Hard to find or one-off pieces
- What it's not good for: Cheaper items and regular stock

Alibaba

Alibaba has become a go-to place for small businesses to get stock. The choice, hands down, beats all other stores.

- What it's good for: price and being able to order large quantities.
- What it's not good for: Little to no protection and you need to order large quantities. The postage can be expensive as most items come from China.

Wish

Like Alibaba but safer. Wish tend to refund if you have a problem. Again, most items come from China so expect some delays in arrival.

- What it's good for: Protection and large stock choice.
- What it's not so good for: Sometimes it feels like there is too much choice.

Places to Find Stock-Specific:

Candles:

Candle Shack : https://candle-shack.co.uk
Sticker Shop : https://www.stickershop.co.uk
Supplies for Candles: https://suppliesforcandles.co.uk
Candlemakers: https://www.candlemakers.co.uk
4Candles: https://www.4candles.co.uk
Randall's Candles: https://www.randallscandles.co.uk
Craftovator: https://www.craftovator.co.uk
Craftastik: https://www.craftastik.co.uk
Trade Essential Oils: https://tradeessentialoils.co.uk

Jewellery:

Blue Streak Crystals: https://tradeessentialoils.co.uk
I-Beads: https://www.i-beads.co.uk

Wholesale Clearance: https://www.wholesaleclearance.co.uk
Jewellery Box: https://www.jewellerybox.co.uk
Jilly Beads: https://www.jillybeads.co.uk
Beads Direct: https://www.beadsdirect.co.uk
Beads: https://www.beads.co.uk
Wholesale Beads: https://www.wholesale-beads.eu

Soap:

Soap Supplier: https://soapsupplier.co.uk
Soap kitchen: https://www.thesoapkitchen.co.uk
Just A Soap: https://justasoap.co.uk
Aromatic Skin Care: https://www.aromantic.co.uk
Grace Fruit: https://www.gracefruit.com
Supplies For Candles: https://suppliesforcandles.co.uk
Soap Makers Store: https://soapmakers-store.com

Fabric and Wool:

Yeomans Yarns: https://yeoman-yarns.co.uk
King Cole: https://www.kingcole.com
Wool Wholesale: https://woolwholesale.com
Wool Warehouse: https://www.woolwarehouse.co.uk
Oddies Textiles: https://www.oddies-textiles.co.uk
Wholesale Fabrics: https://wholesalefabrics.co.uk
Wouters Textiles: https://www.wouters-textiles.com
Fabric Land: https://www.fabricland.co.uk
Pound Fabric: https://poundfabrics.co.uk
The Button Company: https://www.buttoncompany.co.uk

Packaging:

Tiny Box Company: https://www.tinyboxcompany.co.uk
Fold a Box: https://www.foldabox.co.uk
Packing Boxes: https://www.packingboxes.co.uk
Pack Supplies: https://www.pack-supplies.co.uk
Dav Pack: https://www.davpack.co.uk

Before purchasing from any store, make sure you check customer reviews to make sure you dealing with a reputatable company.

12

How do I Work out Costs?

Getting your pricing right when you are setting up will be a case of trial and error. When working out how much you want to charge for each product, you'll need to take three things into consideration:

- 1. Cost to make
- 2. Time it took to make
- 3. Profit you want to make

Cost to Make

These are the costs it takes for each product. You'll need to break down the costs of each item needed to get your product to a customer. I would also include packing materials in this category, although the cost of postage will be met by the customer.

My Example:

- 100 chains -£21.99 (0.22 each)
- 50 jump hoops -£3.65 (0.07 each)

- 42 Large Gems - £9.97 (0.23 x 6=£1.42)
- 200 small gems -£4.25(0.02 each)
- 25 backs-£ 5.97(0.23)
- Glue(100ml)- £6.99 (0.06 each use)
- Stickers (25 pages but can print 36 a page) - £5.99 (0.23 per page / 36 =0.006)
- 100 envelopes -£8.75(0.08 each)
- Bubble wrap 5m -£ 10.99 (0.44 each)
- Cardboard boxes (50)- £6.99 (0.14 each)
- Labels 100 - £2.98(0.03 each)
- Velvet bags (50)-£8.00 (0.16 each)

In order to work out what each necklace costs me to make, I would firstly calculate the cost of each individual part. So, If I buy necklace chains in packs of 100 at £21.99, I need to do the sum: 21.99/100= £0.22. This is the cost of each chain.

If did this sum for all of my necklace parts and packaging items, then my total manufacturing costs would be £2.88 per necklace.

Time It Takes to Make the Product

It is important to know how long it would take you to make an item so you can work out your hourly wage. I know I can make ten necklaces an hour. So, my hourly rate would be:

Profit per necklace x 10 = £ depending on method

The longer it takes you, the more you'll have to charge. If you have a set amount you want to earn per hour, you'll have to factor that into your overall costs. I'd like to make at least £10 an hour. This means my per piece rate is:

60 minutes /£10= £0.16

Profit

There are several ways to calculate your profit. I've listed three common ways:

Add 20/30%

- £2.88 cost of necklace and packaging + 0.16p hourly rate =£3.04
- To account for hosting/extras, I would add an extra 10% =0.30p
- Total is £3.34
- Add 30% = £1.02 this is your profit so you would retail for: £4.36
- (This method is probably more suitable for larger items)

Cost x 3

- £3.04 x 3= £9.12 (profit £6.08)
- For wholesale, it is usually x2 of cost

Add what you want to make.

- If you wanted to make £7 profit per necklace, I would add that to my costs to get my retail price.

- £3.04 +£7= £10.04

Depending on how saturated your market is could mean you have to choose the best pricing module to attract customers. I use the second option in case of sudden price rises. I can still make a decent profit on those figures.

Fees

If you sell on Etsy, you will have to take into account how much Etsy charges you to sell your items on its site.

Currently the fees to sell on Etsy are:

- 0.20p to list an item
- 4% transaction fee
- 4%+0.20p process fee

So, if I chose option 2 (£9.12) my costs would be:
0.20+ 0.36 +0.56=£1.12

Now my total is: £10.24

To work out my total profit=

£10.24 −(£3.04(costs)+£1.12(fees)) =£6.08 per necklace

This means my hourly rate would be:

£6.08 x 10 = £60.80 p/h

(This may seem a lot, but depends on sales and you may not wish to work many hours.)

Here are two sites that do all the math for you:

- https://bgraphics.co.uk (Etsy UK seller fee calculator)
- https://craftybase.com (Etsy seller fee calculator)

https://Percentagecalculator.com is also a good site to have available.

13

How do I Come up With a Good Name?

Picking a name for your business is a bit like choosing a name for your child. You want something that will age well but will also suit the recipient. If you are lucky, you might already have a name you are happy with. If this is the case, feel free to skip to the next chapter. But if you don't, then here are a few ways to help you think of a good name.

On a Piece of Paper Write the Following:

1. What you are selling
2. Key colours you like or are usual in your line of business
3. Industry recognised words
4. Your name or a special name
5. Place where you live
6. Your USP's

So, my list would look like:

1. Necklaces, jewellery, cosplay
2. Pink, green, red
3. Jewellery, gold, pendants
4. Rachael
5. London
6. Quick, cheap, good quality

Run Keywords Through a Business Name Generator

These handy tools combine key words you've supplied as well as their own:

- Oberlo: http://oberlo.co.uk/tools/business-name-generator
- Business Name Generator: https://businessnamegenerator.com
- Shopify: https://www.shopify.com/tools/business-name-generator

What to Do if Your Idea Is Taken?

If you go to register a store on Etsy and the name is taken, it is less of a problem as you can add extra words or numbers to your shop name. most people search Etsy for the product they want, not the shop they want to buy it from.

With a website, it would be best to try and think of a different name or mix up the order of words. So instead or Pink Pendants you could do Pendants in Pink.

Other Suggestions:

- Acronyms: like IKEA (name of founder and town born in).
- Local areas/features: Amazon, the river.
- Use two key words: it's easier to combine two key words than just using one word as this is less likely to have been taken.
- Remove or add letters: if you combine two words or use one word with letters added this can work
- Use a pet or close persons names: I have a business in my daughter's name.
- Literature names: stick to older books so you won't face legal problems. Nike is a clothing brand but also the name of a Greek god.
- Foreign words: great idea if you speak another language. Don't be tempted to use an online translator as these don't always get it right.

How Do I know if It's a Good Name?

- Do you like it?
- It sounds good/looks right?
- You're sure it won't offend someone?
- You want it?

If you answer 'Yes' to all of these, then go for it. If you do hope to expand at a later date, it is worth looking for websites that have similar names and also for registered trademarks. It's easier to find a name that is unique than having to rebrand/face legal action.

14

Workbook: Part Two

Lesson One

- What are your skills? List a minimum of three.
- What are your hobbies? List a minimum of three.
- Do you want to focus on passive income? If yes, what ideas could you use?
- Example: *I could make passive income by writing an eBook or making knitting patterns.*

Brain Dump

- Write down five main ideas you could make a business in. Be vague such as 'sewing' or 'candle making'. What are your five ideas?

Niche Ideas

- For each of these five ideas, write three niche ideas that could be associated with the main ideas. What are your niche ideas for each main idea?

- Example: *If I had written candles as my main idea, I could make it more niche by using unique scents, craving unusual shapes (maybe flowers) or organic materials being used in production.*

Narrowing Down ideas

- Am I passionate about them: which ideas do not inspire me?
- Required skills: which ideas would require a significant investment in time or money to gain more skills to make these products?
- Realistic: is the idea currently achievable in your situation? Which ideas are not?
- What ideas are you left with?

Marketable:

- Is your idea in an over saturated market? Choose three of the niche ideas and research how many items are in each category to find out how many people are selling similar items to your niche idea.
- If there are a lot of similar products, how could you make yours even more unique, so it stands out?
- Now try searching for these new niche ideas you have thought of. Are the results lower?
- If they do have lower results, choose one of the ideas you are the most passionate about starting a business with.
- If the results have not gone down, go back the

previous steps and see if you can change the
ideas to make them more unique.

Lesson Two

Facebook Groups

- What questions could you ask in a business
  minded group? Think of at least two.
- What questions could you ask in a hobby-based
  group? Think of at least two.

Research

- Look at a minimum of five products in your
  category. List five positive comments said in
  reviews.
- Now, list five negative comments said in
  reviews.
- With the five negative comments, what could
  you do to make them into positives?
- Example: *Negative comment about competitors'
  product: Poor quality. Change : You would make high
  quality goods and focus on your quality in your
  descriptions.*

- If you decided to buy products to research:
- Choose two or three products from each price
  point (Low, middle and high). If funds are tight,
  you can compare based on the photographs on
  the seller's page, reviews and descriptions.
- What do you like and dislike about each item?
  How does if differ from yours? Is there
  anything you see from these products that you
  could use to make your product better?

Keywords

- Searching on Etsy, what five key words get suggested in the drop-down bar when you search for items like yours?
- Searching on the web, what five key words get suggested in the drop-down bar when you search for items like yours?

Trending Items

- When you type 'Trending now 'your item'', what are the top three categories? Try this on both Etsy and a search engine.
- Example :
- When I search for trending jewellery, rings, necklaces and bracelets are the three top categories.
- Choose one category. What are the three most popular style or type items in that category?
- Example :
- If I conducted a search for necklaces I would find monogram, emerald (birth month), and gold.
- Which category would your item fit?

Pinterest and Instagram

- What are the popular themes, colours or textures in fashion currently? Search Instagram and Pinterest for fashionable trends.
- Could you adapt your idea to include one of these current trends?

Ideal Customer

- What do you think are the pros and cons of making an item to fit the popular market?
- What do you think are the pros and cons of making an item to fit the niche market?
- Using the example in this chapter in the book, how would you describe your ideal customer?

Unique Selling Point

• What would be your USP?

• What are the pros and cons of your USP's? choose three of the best to use in the next exercise.

• Once you've decided which are best, write three sentences explaining your product and its USP's.

• Can you narrow this description down to a single sentence?

Lesson Three

This plan is designed to be filled out as you progress through the book.

Name of Business:

- What will the business will be called ?

Summary of Business:

- Write a three sentence summary of your business.
- Condense these into a one sentence summary of your business.

Ideal Customer:

- Write a description of your Ideal customer:

Competition:

- Who are your three main competitors?
- Suggest three areas that you are competing in:

USP's:

- What are your unique selling points?

Pricing and Costs:

- What will be your initial set up costs ?
- Which price point you will be selling at (High, middle or low)?

Funding:

- In which ways you will fund your business?

Selling:

- Which places you will sell your items?
- What are the reasons you will use these platforms?
- Will you be selling in person?

Marketing:

- What online platforms will you be marketing in and why have you chosen them?
- If you are selling in person, where would you market and why?

Set Up:

- Are you going to be self-employed or set up a business?
- Explain why you have chosen this option:

Legal:

- What specific insurances will you need for your business?
- Are there specific legislations that apply to your business?
- Do you need to inform other agencies (i.e. the local authority) that you have set up your business?

Lesson Four

- What are the key items of stock that you need?
- What key words can you use to research and find stock?
- Choose three items that you need. Expand and narrow down your key words to see if you get better results.
- Example: *If I wanted to find an 18in gold chain, I would expand that by adding the carat of gold or style of chain I required. If I decided to narrow down, I would just search for gold chains.*
- As well as the example stores given in the corresponding chapter, which other stores could you use? Find five more stores.

Lesson Five

Materials:

Either draw a table or make one in Excel. Add the following columns: item, cost, number of items for cost and cost per individual item (cost / amount of items for cost). Fill in your chart.

Add up the total of costs per individual items to find out how much it would cost to make one item.

Example: *The item is gold chains that cost £21.99 for 100 chains. To get the cost per individual item, I would enter the cost and divide that number by the number of items I got for that cost. This would mean each necklace was £0.21.*

Packing materials:

Make another table. Add the following columns: item, cost, amount of items for cost and cost per individual item(cost/amount of items for cost). Fill in your chart the same way you filled it in for the materials table.

Add up the total costs of costs per individual items to find out how much it would cost to make one item.

- How many items can you make per hour?
- How much profit would you like to make per item?

Profit

Work out your profit using the three different methods below.

Add 20% to cost of individual item

- Costs (item and packing costs) =
- Hourly rate (divide by amount of products you can make per hour)=

- Extras (10% of costs) =
- Total if added together:
- Add 20%=
- Total:

Cost x3

- Add your costs, hourly rate and extras and multiple by three.
- Total:

Pick Your Profit

- Costs, hourly rate and extras. Add the amount of profit you'd like to make per item too.
- Total:

- Which is the most profitable for you to use?
- Which way do you prefer to use?

Fees

To make it simpler, you can use the two websites suggested in the chapter. Otherwise, use this simple sum:

- Total cost (including postage):
- 4% of the above cost:
- (multiply by two as there are two sets of 4% deducted):
- Subtract 0.20p:
- (multiply by two as there are two sets of 0.20p deducted):
- Total of deductions:

Final profit:

- Total paid (including postage) by customer - (postage, fees and costs):

Hourly rate:

- Profit X Amount you can make in an hour:

Lesson Six

Homemade Names Generator

- The place where you live
- Your name or a name close to you
- Your USP
- The name of item you are selling
- Associated key colours
- An Industry recognised name

Online Generator

- List your eight favourite names from an online generator
- If your ideal name is taken, what ways could you change the name so that you could use it?

Other Suggestions (list one idea for each)

- Use an acronym
- Your local area or a famous feature
- Two key words
- Remove or add letters
- A name from literature
- A Foreign word or phrase

Business Name

- What business name have you decided to use?
- What three parts of this chapter have been the most helpful to you?

End of Chapter Questions

- Which three parts of this chapter have been the most helpful to you?
- Choose one thing from this chapter that you could use and implement today. What have you chosen and how are you going to implement it?

PART III

Branding

15

How Will You Present Yourself?

Back Story:

- This is important in places like Etsy as buyers like to know who they are buying from.
- Your back story can be short and can lead into several paragraphs. You are trying to let buyers know that your products are made by a real person.
- You'll want to highlight why you are unique. Perhaps mention why your USP's are important to you.
- You'll also want to show your ethics. Are you Eco Conscious? Mention it.

Colours:

- Be mindful of your audience. If you are aiming at men, picking stereotypical feminine colours will put some men off.

- The colours you use should both look good in print and on the web.
- For specific colours use Hex Codes (HTML colour codes). http://colour-hex.com has a wide selection of colours. If you are working with a designer, it is far easier to give them hex codes than examples of colours you like as hex codes are exact matches.
- Hex codes appear as a hash with letters and numbers relating to a colour. So 'Salmon Pink' would be #ff9999
- Another good website to find colour combinations is https://colorhunt.co .The site shows you combinations of colours that work well together so you can develop a colour palette.

Typography:

- There is an art to picking letters that just work well together.
- It's important to maintain the same styles over your whole brand to maintain consistency. Pinterest offer great examples of this. Creative Market also suggest packages of styles that work well together. You can also have a ready-made logo designed using two fonts you like.
- https://fontjoy.com and https://fontpair.co combine two different fonts for you.
- creativebloq.com has good articles on font parings that work well.
- Experiment with height and bold settings to set visual hierarchy. Much like in paragraphs, you

will display certain words more prominently than others to signify their importance over less significant words.

Logos:

- When you have both the colours and typography that you want, you can now have a go at making a logo. You can make your own in Photoshop, but this requires significant skill and is something professionals take time to learn. There are programmes such as Canva which are free or Vista Print which you pay for that will make a logo for you, but it will be fairly generic.
- The next step is to approach a designer on places such as Etsy or creative market. They will sell the same design several times but will be happy to make small adjustments such as font or colour. Other places to try are Fiverr and Upwork.
- The final option is to commission a one-off logo. This can be expensive and not something I would do unless you feel it's vital to your brand at this stage.

Tag-lines:

- Remember in Chapter Two where you had to summarise your business into a sentence? This is the essence of your tagline. Most large companies will have a tagline. From supermarkets to computers, it is a way for companies to get you to remember them and sometimes show what it is they stand for. These aren't essential, many businesses don't have them. If you feel you want one, try using a tagline for a few weeks and see if you think it works.

- Use one sentence as a starting point. If you can get it shorter, i.e. a word, even better.

Branding Board:

- Once you have your colours, typography and logo, you can make a branding board. Pinterest is full of ideas of ways to layout a branding board. Branding boards help you keep consistency in your brand and save you time by having all the Hex codes, typography names and your colour palette all in one place.

16

Photography

In order to sell your products successfully, you will need to ensure you have high quality photographs. You don't need an expensive camera or high-end kit in order to take good pictures. I use a small light box from Amazon and iPhone for all of my images.

What Makes a Good Picture?

- Good lighting- no dark shadows
- Related props
- Clean backgrounds
- Complementary colours
- Item is clear and presented well
- Cropped if needed.

What Makes a Bad Picture?

- Dark shadows

- Unrelated props
- Messy or distracting backgrounds
- Non-complementary colours
- Poorly cropped photo

Tips for Better Photographs:

- Look at Your Competitors. Is there a theme in the photographs in your category? In jewellery for example, I've seen lots of sellers showcase their items on models. It's also common to use a ruler or penny to show the size of the item in one of the pictures shown at the end of the carousel. If you are selling handmade candles, then you might use flowers as props to feed into the idea of a natural product.
- Include Detail. This is particularly important if your item has interesting or eye-catching detail. A clear, zoomed in picture of an interesting detail can appeal to buyers who are impressed with detail. Shows that your items are handmade and also top quality.
- Don't Clutter Your Image. One relevant and well-placed prop is better than four or five poorly placed ones. Remember that you are using a prop to showcase your item not to act as a distraction. If you are unsure of using a prop but want to display your item in a more interesting manner, then consider using items such as boxes with fabric draped over them or items such a logs or jewellery trees. Get creative.
- Get the Right Equipment. As I said earlier, you

don't need to spend loads of money on light boxes or cameras. If you have a modern smartphone you can take decent pictures on that.

- Backgrounds. I bought a small light box for £8.99. it allows me to have a little light behind my products that really makes them sparkle. You can buy bigger versions of light boxes depending on your need. If you can't stretch to a huge box, consider using large sheets of paper/card and make your own. Sticking two large sheets of card together to make an 'L' shape is cheap. You can experiment with backgrounds and use different coloured ones depending on your products. It is best to develop a consistent theme in all your photographs. Stick to your colour palette so your images are recognisable.
- Photo Editing Software. Most of the time I use Apple's built in photo editing software. but there are also several great apps such as Camera +, Snapseed and Tadaa which also do a great job
- Light is Your Friend. if you don't have enough natural light your photographs can end up looking low quality. Blurry and grainy photos will not tempt customers. Using flash in an attempt to solve this problem can in fact make it worse. Shadows and distorted colours will leave you with both an unattractive and unrealistic item. To solve these issues its best to shoot your pictures in natural light (morning is best) and using a light background to attract more light to your pictures.
- Blurry and Unfocused Images. To get people to

buy your product, you need to have some professional pride in your work. Posting blurry and unfocused images makes it harder for the customer to see the quality of your work which means they are less likely to buy from you. This is a really easy fix. If using your phone, check if you are able to use a focus option. On my phone, I am able to tap the screen to focus. Cameras usually have this option too, but you will need to check your manual to find out how to do it.

I would highly recommend spending a decent amount of time looking at how people style their photographs. You don't just have to stick to your type of product. you can get lots of ideas from looking outside your niche.

17

Packaging

Presenting your product in attractive packaging is just as important as spending time on your product. There are several elements to consider in packaging. While high quality packaging is desirable, you don't have to spend a fortune. Small details such as twine or ribbon with a note attached are inexpensive but will add an extra touch. There are several companies that offer a wide range of packaging material:

- Tinybox
- Foldabox
- Packing boxes
- Pack supplies
- Dav Pack
- Amazon
- eBay

You'll want to make sure you don't get any boxes that are too large as this increases the postage costs for you. Whatever you choose also needs to protect your product. I have had a few orders turn up broken which not only costs me money but is also hugely disappointing for a customer. I make sure I use bubble wrap around my necklaces to ensure they are protected as well as using a padded envelope. It's better to spend a little more time and money on packaging that is secure as your item is less likely to get broken that way.

Branding your packaging is one way to distinguish your product. It is also a good way for the recipient of your product to find you again should they want to place a further order. Stickers are something I've used on the pillow boxes that I place my necklaces in. I put one sticker on the front with my logo and another on the back with my shop name. Should one of my necklaces be given as a gift, then the recipient can easily search for me.

Business cards are also something I have included in my parcels. As I have a Facebook page and website, I find it handy to be able to give details of these to customers for future reference. A twist on the business card is to add your brand story on the back of the card If it will fit. If a customer is interested in finding out more, they can then go on your website and see your other stock.

When you start making a decent amount of money, you might consider looking at custom packaging. This is where your logo is printed directly onto a box or envelope. If your items aren't that expensive, then it isn't worth it but if you sell mid-high range items, then this can make you appear more professional.

Offering gift wrapping can also distinguish you from your competition. Wrapping paper and ribbon are fairly inexpensive and the process requires little effort. I would do this for all orders over Christmas and also if the delivery address was different from the buyers.

Avoiding breakages should be a top priority for you as a seller. Why spend ages on a product to only have it broken? There are a wide range of products to protect your item. Bubble wrap is a standard way to protect delicate items and is malleable so easy to fit around oddly shaped items. Maize pellets are an environmentally friendly item to choose should that fit with your ethics. It can be composted after use so less waste goes to a landfill. Shredded paper is also good for you as it reduces your waste. It is also less damaging than plastic. Obviously be careful with what you shred - No bank records. If you have large items that need extra padding, you can use bubble cushions. They won't offer great protection for items that may break easily, however. Paper items can be placed into a card backed envelope so that you don't have a bent item arriving at your buyer's door. Make sure to add a Do Not Bend sticker.

When making up your parcels, it is important to make sure you add some key information for your buyer in with any extras. Items to include might be:

- Business cards
- Freebies. Depending on your product, a free item that is related to your product will always go down well. If you sell jewellery, some inexpensive earrings might be appropriate. Wax melts would be a good option for candles and a small needle holder could be helpful if you sell needle crafts. If you make paper goods, then a nice bookmark will cost you next to nothing to make but will be appreciated.
- Discount Codes. You can send these via email after your buyer has ordered from you. I've always found including one in the package as part of a thank you note gets me better results. For an added bonus, you can add a code that can be given to a friend should they want one.

Offering free shipping or a small free item also offers the same sort of thing.

- Receipt/Invoice. We should all try to reduce our waste, so this isn't necessary, but it is good practice, especially for a high value item. If the item is being shipped internationally, it is also a good idea should the parcel be stopped by customs.
- How to Look After Your Item. If your item requires special care, a small sheet containing some advice will be appreciated by your customers. This also reduces complaints in the case of buyers not knowing how to care for their new purchase.

There are several methods you can consider when wrapping your product for shipping. For sturdy or soft items, a plastic mailer bag is a good option as it flexible. This isn't so good for small items as there is too much room to move around which increases the chance of damage. Display boxes are a nice touch to impress your customer. It saves time wrapping and looks professional if given as a gift. Expensive items are more suitable for this method as, due to the cost, a cheaper item would not be worth using one of these boxes for. Add some tissue paper and ribbon and you have a high-end gift. Plain shipping boxes for items with their own display boxes add that extra level of protection. Damaging a display box will ruin your customers experience. Another option is pillow boxes which are good for jewellery and very small items. As they are fairly sturdy, they can offer extra protection. Padded envelopes can be used with many other items to give extra packaging protection. These can be bought in large quantities and are cheap.

Setting up a packaging station is something I highly recommend, making your life easier. You might not have a huge amount of space: all you need is a box with all your packing supplies that is easy to handle and use. You should include:

- Scissors
- Packing tape
- Scales
- Choice of packaging
- Items to go in packs (invoices, business cards and freebies etc)
- Return address labels (essential for all parcels should they get lost)
- Custom labels if shipping abroad
- Labels to write addresses on

If shipping internationally then you will need to fill in a custom label. Ensure you have the correct weight, item name and value and that the declaration has been completed or your item can be rejected and sent back.

Shipping Times

Being able to ship quickly will be a huge incentive to some customers. Even offering expedited shipping will attract some more. Be honest in your shipping times as if you lie, you'll get bad reviews and lose customers. Its best to under promise and over deliver when it comes to retail as the customer tends to be happier. Make sure you write your shipping policies clearly on your selling platform so that customers are aware of your shipping times when ordering.

I would also try to get into a regular routine in regard to going to the post office, so you don't have to go out every day. I tend to post Monday, Wednesday and Friday unless someone has paid for expedited shipping.

18

Workbook: Part Three

Lesson One

Colour Palette

Choose two websites (high-end/big company). Look at their colour palette.

- What are the main colours they use on their site and branding materials?
- What colours might you use for your business (include Hex codes if you know them)?
- Using the colour palette website mentioned in the chapter, create a colour palette for your business.

Backstory

- What would you like customers to know about you (i.e. why you make your items and your process)?
- Why might they want to know this?

- How has your backstory affected your company's USP's?

Typography

- Find three brands you admire and study their typography. What do you like and dislike about their typography?
- Using the websites listed in the chapter, choose three combinations that you think you would like to use in your business.
- Why have you chosen these three combinations?
- Which one do you think would suit your business best?

Logo

- Think of a logo you have seen that you believe would suit your business. What is it about the logo that appeals to you?
- Is there anything you would change about that logo if it was for your business?
- What key features would you like your logo to have? Think whether you want it line based, using certain colours or if you have a particular image in mind.
- In your notebook, sketch out three logo designs you could use for your business.
- Choose your favourite design. How well would it transfer onto a printed document or website? Could you make it simpler and more easy to recognise?
- In your notebook, sketch out three variations of

your favourite design. You could make a more detailed or simplistic version for example.

Tagline

- What are the tag lines for McDonald's, Apple and Tesco?
- Can you think of a five word tagline for your business?
- Could you make it shorter such as with Nike which is three words?
- Where will you place your tagline? Could you incorporate it into your logo or will you have it as a separate item?

Lesson Two

- What props do your competitors use? Do they stick to a certain type of prop?
- Is there a theme to photographs in your sales categories?
- What props could you use in your photographs?
- Take a few photographs with your props. Which items worked and which didn't?
- Why do think some props worked and some didn't?
- Where in your home is best for taking photographs? Experiment by taking a few photographs in different rooms of your home at different times of the day.
- What is your ideal location in your home for photographs?
- What is the ideal time?

Packaging

- Think of a few examples of good quality packaging. These might have been products you have received. Why did you like the packaging?
- Where could you source packaging materials locally?
- Where could you source packaging materials online?
- Are your items easily breakable?
- How could you protect your item from damage such as from water or being dropped?
- Which ways of packaging your product would you use?
- What other ways could you pack your items creatively?

Branding

- How could you brand your packaging?
- Which do you think is the best way to brand your packaging? (You should consider cost, your own skills and time.)

Inside the Parcel

- As well as the examples given in the chapter, what other items would you need to include in your parcels?

Packing Space

- What area would you use to pack your items?

- What would you have in your space?
- How much will it cost to you buy/make your packaging per individual item?

End of Chapter Questions

- Which three parts of this chapter have been the most helpful to you?
- Choose one thing from this chapter that you could use and implement today. What have you chosen and how are you going to implement it?

PART IV

Selling

19

Selling Platforms

The great thing about handmade products is that you have several options when it comes to selling. Gone are the days where you could only make money selling in person at fairs. Now you also have an option to sell on your own website or on an online marketplace such as Etsy. For each option, I'll give you the pros and cons so you can make up your mind on which would suit you and your products best.

Keywords

- Hosting company: The company whose servers your website is hosted on. I.e. Site Ground.
- Domain name: This is your 'www.' Address. You can buy these from domain registers such as Namecheap.
- SEO: Key words that are linked to your site that someone might use to find you on somewhere like Google.

- Plugin: Add extra uses to your website. Forms, payment buttons as well as backup plugins are available.

Websites: Benefits

Complete Control

With a website, you can choose how you design the site, how you market the site and can customise views to your site with Search Engine Optimisation (SEO). You can add all sorts of nifty extras such as email sign up as well as offering a range of payment options. There are also very few rules that you'd have to abide by, so you don't have to fear being shut down for breaking a policy. As long as you don't break your hosting company's policies, then you will be fine.

Professionalism

Having your own website shows a certain level of commitment to a buyer. Spending time and money on a website will lead to more sales as customers will start to recognise you as a brand.

Expandability

If you want to make your business bigger, having your own website will allow this. It will be easier to contact journalists or make adverts if you have a website and you'll be taken more seriously. You are also not limited by extra fees or competing with others, like you would be on somewhere like Etsy.

. . .

You Can Talk to Customers Directly

The great thing about having a website is that you can obtain your customers email address and promote other products or ask for feedback. Offering an incentive such as free shipping or a discount code will entice buyers to sign up to your email list. Make sure you comply with GDPR, which will be covered later in this book.

Website: Costs

The Buck Stops With You.

With all that freedom comes responsibility. If you have an unfair review or your site goes down, it's on you to fix it. Your new role is not only the role of artisan but also marketing director and customer service representative.

You'll Need to Invest Time

Learning how to construct even a basic website will take time. It took me two weeks to find out how to make my own website; most of that was spend learning how to link PayPal to my website. I laugh about it now as it isn't really that hard, it's more a case of having to complete several steps at the same time or nothing seems to work. There are a plethora of blogs that walk you through how to set up your website.

Cost

You will have to budget for costs such as domain names, site hosting and also payment fees. Being good at juggling your cash flow will be a skill you will soon pick up.

. . .

How to Set Up a Website

Wix

- https://www.quicksprout.com/how-to-make-a-wix-website/
- https://www.youtube.com/watch?v=JTdK9q_iuE0

Square space

- https://www.websitebuilderexpert.com/website-builders/squarespace/how-to-use-squarespace/
- https://support.squarespace.com/hc/en-us/articles/205809798-Video-Series-Getting-Started-with-Squarespace

WordPress

- https://websitesetup.org
- https://www.youtube.com/watch?v=2cbvZf1jIJM

Both Wix and Square Space are very simple to use - what you see is what you get. You can drag text boxes to where you want them and add lots of effects with no coding experience.

WordPress requires a little more technical knowledge, but to date I have always been able to find the solution to my problem via a quick google search. You can expand your site more easily with WordPress and there are more external plug-ins able to work within it.

. . .

There are many websites available to help you compare hosting and domain registering companies. Do make sure the author is not being offered commission as this may make them biased.

Hosting Companies/Domain Registers

Most hosting sites will also offer you the chance to register your domain with them at the same time. You can move your domain and hosting once your contract expires, which is typically a year unless you pay for longer.

Here are a few well known hosting and domain registering companies:

- Lyrical Host
- Site ground
- Bluehost
- Name cheap
- Go Daddy
- Ionos

Etsy: Benefits

You are Under a Trusted Brand

As you are selling from an already established brand, buyers are going to feel far more secure in handing over their payment details. Buyers will also be aware of the added protection in buying from a seller on Etsy as opposed to someone on another less well known website.

. . .

Easy Set Up

You can set up and be selling on Etsy in less than an hour. Apart from your shop name and logo, there is very little else design wise to sort out.

Benefit of Etsy's Marketing Budget

Etsy is a large company with an equally large budget. They can afford to spend money advertising in order to attract people to Etsy who in turn spend money in shops like yours. If you had to be solely responsible for advertising, then it would cost you a significant amount of money.

No Cost Set Up

Yes, you do have to pay fees, but it won't cost you a penny to set up your store. Etsy is soon to roll out subscriptions which would require sellers to pay to use Etsy in exchange for extra benefits. They will still have a free model, but this will be fairly basic.

Support

Etsy has a great forum in which you can ask questions and find reliable answers. You are also able to call Etsy should you have a problem.

Etsy: Issues

Hard to Be an Individual

Lots of listings look the same and buyers rarely search for items based on a shop name. You will have to work very hard to stand out.

. . .

Newer Items are at the Top

Etsy regularly change their algorithms so you can never be sure where your item may appear on a search (unless you pay for ads). You will have to accept that items that are newer than yours or that have paid money for adverts, will appear above your own items. This means that all of your great descriptions and amazing products may not be seen by your ideal customers. This is why it is important to use the correct keywords that buyers use to search when setting up your listing.

Google Can Be Fickle With Etsy

Unlike having your own website, where you can improve your listings SEO, with Etsy you are at the mercy of both google and Etsy themselves. As there is a push for people to pay to appear higher up in search pages, you may find yourself left behind if you don't do this.

All Your Eggs are in One Basket

Etsy can remove your listings or your shop for any reason and you can't do anything about it. While this is rare, if you rely on this income, then this can be very daunting.

Fees

Etsy charge you fees to list your products and also once you have sold your products. While you will be charged a payment processing fee on your website, you'll need to compare the cost of theses versus Etsy's costs to see which would be cheaper for you.

· · ·

How to Set Up an Etsy Shop

- https://www.howtogeek.com/369907/how-to-set-up-an-etsy-shop/
- https://help.etsy.com/hc/en-gb/articles/115015672808-How-to-Open-a-Shop?segment=selling
- https://startups.co.uk/how-to-start-an-etsy-shop/

In Person: Benefits

You Can Go Into Detail About Your Product

If your buyer wants to extra details or has a question, you can answer them instantly.

Easier to Upsell

When you have a buyer in front of you wanting to buy a necklace, it is far easier to show them the matching earrings or bracelet as you are literally right in front of them. Unless you specifically design your website to include areas on listings to show what other people also bought, then you could have missed your chance.

Building Relationships

Interacting with the seller and being able to physically hold the item builds trust with a customer. If a buyer likes your work, they will be interested in your other pieces and will look out for your next designs.

In Person: Issues

Limited Market

If you have a niche product, you may struggle to sell it to the general population. It doesn't matter if you are in busy area with lots of people passing by; if you don't have what they want, they won't buy from you. If you are able to adapt pieces to be more marketable alongside niche items, this can solve the problem.

Fees

Depending on your contract, you may have to pay either a flat fee or percentage of sales. If you have to pay a flat fee, this will be payable even if you don't sell anything.

Time

It is time consuming selling on a stall. You can spend several hours at a location and have no orders. If you invested that sort of time on your online business, you are far more likely to see a return.

Tips for Selling at Fairs

- https://blog.folksy.com/2015/11/03/essential-craft-fair-checklist
- https://hearthookhome.com/beginners-craft-fair-tips-how-to-run-a-successful-craft-show-booth/

If you are interested in testing your idea with limited commitment, then an Etsy store would be the best place to start. It's low cost and low risk with a large ready-made audience so you don't have to spend time or money advertising. Selling niche but generally acceptable items, such as unique candles, would work on any of the selling platforms listed. Even people who care about eco-friendly candles, might be tempted if they like the fragrance.

20

How to Get Paid

Which payment method you accept will differ depending on where you are selling.

In Person

A PayPal card reader could be the right choice for you. PayPal is one of the biggest payment processing companies and well known. Much like you would pay for goods in a high street store, you get a small card reader and can take payments from buyers when they enter their pin. You don't see the payment details so customers can be reassured that they are not going to be scammed. There is no fixed contract to use this service and you pay a fee on sales. The fees range from 1% to 2.75% of the sale and you will need an internet connection.

iZettle is another card reading company that you should look into if you are selling in person. There is a flat fee of 1.75% on all transactions and they have fairly quick deposit times. You also have the option of having a till module attached so if you sell lots of different items, you don't need to keep entering codes or prices as they are already there. This can also help with stock management. You would need to make sure this is something you would utilise as otherwise there is no point paying extra for it.

If you would like a free eCommerce website, then Square is a card reader you could consider. As well as a free website, they also offer an app you can use to take payments via your phone. This method also applies to people calling you to place orders. The company also offer lots of extra freebies to help you succeed. There is a £29 charge to set up as well as a 1.75-2.5% fee on all sales.

Sum Up is set up via an app on your tablet or phone. There is no monthly cost and there is a fairly low fee rate of 1.69% on all orders. There are no extra freebies as this is a very basic set up with only a £19 charge to start.

Committing to a card reader when you first start out may not be something you are comfortable with. If you are sure you'll have an internet connection at the venue, you can have people pay you directly to your PayPal business account. All the buyer needs are their phone and your email address. It can however be cumbersome and if there is a problem, you have to sort it out, which means you may have to delay processing another sale from another customer. Also, if you don't provide a postage receipt, the transaction can be disputed.

Direct bank transfers work much like using your PayPal email address, except this time you are using your bank instead. Most people have banking apps on their phone now, so this is a very simple process. There is usually no extra fee but check the terms and conditions for your bank. The downside is that customers can be nervous about giving banking details out and your bank may suspend your account temporarily if it sees lots of unusual trans-actions.

Cash is of course another option to use. It is instant and most people have some cash to hand. You also have the added benefit of paying no fees to use it, unlike other options. You will, of course, have to have a safe area to store the cash as well as making sure you have enough spare change to process payments. Accepting just cash can mean you miss out on purchases using card payments so it would be wise to look at accepting both.

Online Payment Methods

PayPal is a large and established business that people trust to process their payments. It isn't hard to add a PayPal button to your site that can also be used on mobile devices. The fees can be high when selling online so this might not be the best option for you.

World Pay is another well-known payment processing company. They accept a variety of currencies as well as cards and PayPal. You need to get a quote for the fees as these are will be personalised to your business.

Shopify is a complete e-commerce platform that offers payment systems too. You can set up a website with Shopify, so you don't have to worry about learning how to add payment methods to your site. The fees can be expensive as you have both transaction and monthly fees. The payoff for this is that everything is included.

Stripe offers extras such as direct debit payments and is fairly reasonable when it comes to fees. You will still need a website but there are no hidden fees. Set up can be challenging if you are new to Stripe and fees take vary in processing time.

Sage Pay can be used both on and offline with no transaction fees. phone payments can also be accepted using this system. If you don't have the technological skills to set up Sage Pay, then you may need to hire someone to help. There is also a higher one-off set up fee to pay so you'll need to decide which would benefit you, transaction fees or a larger one-off cost.

Whatever option you choose, make sure you compare everything each company offers you to see which suits your business best. Large transaction fees might not bother you if you get a lot of extras for your money, but you might prefer to use a simpler payment option with no extras, but which is available at a cheaper price.

How to Add a PayPal Button to Your Website

- https://www.youtube.com/watch?v=iVzQEf0IEYE
- https://internet.com/ecommerce/how-to-add-paypal-to-your-website/

21

Workbook: Part Four

Lesson One

- What are the pros and cons to setting up your business on Etsy?
- What are the pros and cons to setting up your business on a website?
- What are the pros and cons to setting up your business in person?
- Which three would you start selling on? Why have you decided this?

Lesson Two

Complete amble research on your options as choosing a poor one can be costly.

- If your business focuses solely on in-person transactions, which payment method would suit your business?

- What would be the pros and cons of using a fully built in e-commerce system for you?
- What would be the pros and cons of using a separate website and payment system?
- Do you plan to have a fully built in e-commerce solution (such as with Shopify) or do you intend to have a separate website and payment system? Why?

End of Chapter Questions

- Which three parts of this chapter have been the most helpful to you?
- Choose one thing from this chapter that you could use and implement today. What have you chosen and how are you going to implement it?

PART V

Marketing

22

SEO

SEO (Search Engine Optimisation) is the process of optimising your website for search engines such as Google. it is an ongoing process and one you will need to do regularly to make sure your business appears in search engines.

Up to 93% of customers find an item to buy via a search engine (*Forrester Imoz*) so being able to make it easy for a customer to find you is the ultimate goal. To do that, you need to be near the top of the searches. You can pay to do this but for a small business this is unachievable. The other way is to focus on key words.

The ways in which a search engine place you nearer the top is by scanning your website to find how relevant you are. This is achieved through looking at your keywords and phrases. The closer your webpage reflects what a customer typed into a search engine to find the product they desire, the higher your ratings. Customers sometimes misspell names of products or use a term that differs from the norm so be sure to add these into your tags.

You don't have to think of all the key words yourself. Google AdWords is a helpful tool that will help you identify key words for your market.

Linking to other websites will also greatly improve your listings as you will be deemed trustworthy. Search engines monitor how many people click on to your website as well as how many people click out via links. As you have limited control over how many people click to access your website, you have to focus on links out of your website. If you mention the name of another website or brand, simply add a hyperlink so a viewer can click out. Also, make sure you have links to other parts of your site on each page, so you are linking internally too. You'll notice that some websites have all the links at the bottom of every page. This is to help improve their listing results. The more links within your website, the more a search engine will trust you.

If you decide to use social media, link those to your website too. Most websites now include a share button for social media outlets in their themes. SEO isn't scary. It's essential. All you have to do is produce relevant content that is as close as possible to what your buyers will be looking for.

Step By Step Guide to SEO

1. Find Out What People are Searching For. What are the keywords your customers use to find similar products to the one you are selling? Use Google AdWords to search for key words or conduct your own research using a search engine to see what other sellers are using as their keywords.
2. Find Common Search Terms. These are the exact phases used by customers to find your product I.e. 'Rose scented candle'. These will most likely send people to your site as they are

common. Google Trends is good for this type of work.

3. Check Out Your Competition. Using these key phases, who comes up first, second and third in listings? What keywords have they used that differ from yours?

4. Put the Keywords in Key Places. You'll have to make sure your headers (1,2 and 3) have the key words or phrases on as many pages as possible. You'll need to write this information in as many places as possible, include descriptions, titles and blog (if you have one on the site). Don't just randomly insert these words into your work as readers will soon get bored and move on. Create good content that people want to read so the keywords and phrases sound natural.

5. Link Everywhere. As I said earlier, Google ranks you by how many people link to you. You'll need internal links (those that link inside your websites such as the home page) and those that link externally (such as social media or brands).

You can also look at the drop-down menus on places like Etsy or Google to find examples of what people have searched for recently. Start typing the name of your product and see what is suggested. I would also suggest adding misspellings of key words if it's a common mistake. Don't put them in descriptions or titles but in areas such as 'Tags' or 'Key Words' as these won't be obvious to a customer. Misspellings look unprofessional.

23

Social Media

In the past selling was simpler. You would sell in person or via an advert as these were the two options available to you. Now with the rise of social media, you have a variety of ways to market your business without coming across as presumptuous. Customers like engaging with brands they follow, it makes them feel part of a club. Different social media outlets appeal to varying demographics of people. As a seller, it is up to you to find which yields the most returns for your effort.

Facebook- Focus on Writing

Most people you will meet have a Facebook page. The level they engage with Facebook will vary though. Some people are using it religiously while others barely engage at all. You are going to have to try to keep someone coming back to your page and remain interested in what you sell.

Facebook allows you, as business to set up 'Pages' about your shop. You can add your logo to the shop and add product information to the page. You can also add a 'Shop Now' button to direct customers to your website if you don't want to run your shop through Facebook. A Facebook shop suits some sellers as it is very simple to set up. You are, however, at the mercy of Facebook and should you displease them your content can be removed.

The key to keeping people engaged is to add value. If you make candles, you show your process or offer tips on how to make them. Answer your audiences' questions and engage with them. Don't be faceless.

You can also publish adverts through Facebook (and from Facebook to Instagram). These are great for new products or to promote your shop in general. I've always had good engagement and an increase in sales when I have used adverts. I tend get better results when I advertise my whole shop rather than just one item. I believe it's because potential customers can look at my other listings. To grab someone's attention you'll need a good quality image that entices people to click on it. Along with this, you'll need to have a well written pitch. Don't feel you have to go overboard on your writing as no one wants to read several pages of information about any product. A small paragraph that includes your USP's should suffice.

You can find more information about setting up a shop here : www.facebook.com/business/help

Instagram Adverts- Focus on an Image

Instagram is a great place to get your products seen. To have a realistic chance to get any sales from Instagram, you'll need to invest a considerable amount of time in your videos or photographs. Innovative or interesting ways of displaying your products will increase the likelihood of people clicking on your image. There are several different types of adverts:

- Story adverts appear among your customers own stories.
- Photo adverts are standard adverts with an image and text.
- Video adverts feature a video with text attached.
- Carousel adverts include several images in one advert.
- Collection adverts include a group of videos or images in one square image. These are good for linking similar products together.

Instagram also allows you to tailor to your audience to things as specific as look-alike audiences. These are people who act in a similar way to your target audience.

Pinterest- Great if You Add Value

Pinterest is good for images and useful information that can be found on websites or blogs. For people to click your pin, you have to:

- Offer something they want to buy. Your adverts should focus on images that show the item being used or worn and where the viewer can buy the item.

- Offer some information they may want. If you want people to click to visit your shop, you might do an advert on a relevant topic. If you sell handmade bags, you could do a post on what you keep in your bag or how to accessorise an outfit with your bag.

Like Instagram, Pinterest have several advert options.

- Promoted via pin means that your advert is shown as a pin when someone is browsing.
- Promoted carousel involves several images in one carousel. You can have up to five.
- App pins allow viewers to download an app by clicking on a link directly from Pinterest.

Twitter - for the Short and Snappy

Twitter allows you to promote your adverts in two ways once you have set up an advertising account with them.

Promote Mode

All of your tweets made from the account will be advertised, in the hope of increasing your followers. You set it up and it runs for a small fee. You are able to track how well the adverts are doing and can post up to 10 tweets per day per advert campaign.

Promote a Single Tweet

Broken down into several categories, each is set up to appeal to different viewers. If you opt for tweet enjoyment, you will aim to have people re-tweet and respond to your initial tweet. Should you choose to increase your followers, then you would choose the followers option. Website clicks can be an option if you want your website to gain more traffic. And finally, app installs can be used if you have an app you want people to download.

Twitter adverts are run like an auction. So you bid how

much you will pay for each interaction, which could be a click, a response or retweet.

Etsy- Google Shopping and Paid Adverts

While strictly speaking, Etsy isn't a social media platform, it's important to be aware that you can pay to display adverts here. If you pay for Google Shopping adverts, your product will appear in Google's shopping area when people search for your item. You pay per click a person makes. Google tracks if that click results in a sale. you also have the option of promoted listings which pushes your item to the top of the pile when people search for you within Etsy.

With all social media adverts, the cost doesn't need to be high if you have a well defined target audience and a well written advert. I have paid as little as £19 for several days' worth of adverts on Facebook and had a significant increase in sales. Experiment with your target audience if your social media platform allows you to. Focus on platforms that fit with your business and don't feel like you need to use all of them, two will be fine.

24

Local Markets

While a lot of your business maybe conducted online, selling on a stall at a fair can give you a great confidence boost and help you hone your selling techniques. Being able to answer a customer question directly will make it easier for you to write your descriptions and policies, as you'll know the sort of information your customers want and what appeals to them.

Selling in person can be nerve-wracking. You may have several worries , so I hope to clarify the two most common issues below.

What if No One Turns Up or I Don't Get Any Sales?

This is a horrible situation to be in, but I've always been a great believer in turning negative experiences into a Positive Learning Experience (PLE). What can you learn from this? Maybe you could change how your items are displayed? Could you be more outgoing? Was your branding consistent? Did you have a banner to distinguish yourself from other sellers? Are you selling to the right audience? Remember that you are the CEO of everything in your business; no one else is going to make items or sell them for you. It's okay to go home, have a cry but it's important to get back on the horse. Go to your next fair with changes in place.

What If I am Asked an Awkward Question?

This is another chance to look for a Positive Learning Experience. The great thing about being in front of someone is that you have to think quickly. I've had some unusual questions asked such as 'Does the necklace come with the (£200) music box?'. The customer was disappointed, even though I assumed most people would know a £15 necklace wouldn't come with a £200 box! I turned the exchange to my advantage. I started including a few links of where to buy the box from that would be easy to notice. If the encounter happens online, you can offer to send a discount code should they wish to buy the necklace. I've always put something like 'I hope you are able to source the music box and here is 10% off to help towards the cost'. Customers will always ask unusual questions; it's your job to answer them without getting flustered. Make a note of questions you are asked regularly and how you respond. This can become crib sheet should you need it again. Ways to find out about local fairs include:

- Local Newspaper
- Local Newspaper online
- Local Leaflets
- Specific industry magazines
- Local Facebook groups
- Specific industry events
- Council newsletters

If you are attending an event, make sure you mention this on your social media platform as you never know who is in the area and might want to come along.

Preparing For a Fair

- Make Enough Stock. Make a few of each of your range as samples for people to test. You'll need to make enough stock so that people can buy on the day. If you run out of stock, have some discount codes that you can hand out. You could even offer to order the items online for the customer there and then if you have a store. I would also take a folder with some images of your other products and leave them on display for potential customers to view. Again, offer a code to encourage someone to pay now and receive later.
- Decide on Your Payment Method. As discussed in Chapter Four, this is a personal choice. Make sure you have it set up and know how it works.
- Displays. How will you display your items? Layering items on plinths or boxes can make your display look less like a car boot table and draw buyers to your stall. How can you stand out? Do you have enough brand promoters such as a banner? Make sure you have information cards on each item that include its name, price and a short description.
- How Will You Cope With Being at a Stall? It can be boring sitting and waiting for customers. You can also look disinterested if you start reading a magazine. One way to look engaged is to make your products in front of customers.

You get to show off your skills and also make it easier to talk to customers. If you have something that can't be made on the day, try demonstrating packing the item in front of customers. You'll look productive and save time at home.

- Packing. How will you present your goods? You can either invest in packaging that is high quality but could take a while to make up, or opt for something cheap and easy. It depends on your brand. You can always have a few items pre-wrapped and ready to go. If you want to be super organised, use different wrapping colours or ribbon so you can easily pick up the right item.

25

Other Marketing

In addition to social media, there are other viable ways to market your business which should appeal to your customers. Never appear impatient, always be courteous and helpful. You catch more flies with honey than with vinegar.

Coupons/Discount Emails/Newsletters

Etsy do not allow you to send marketing emails directly to customers. You can include an opt in bonus such as 20% off if they sign up for a newsletter, or place a business card in your parcels, but not via mail. If you sell via your own website, you are free to do this as long as you comply with GDPR. Your customer must activity opt in to sign up. That means they have to tick a box to agree. you can't ask them to opt out. To get people to give you their details, you have to offer something really appealing. A complimentary item, free shipping or a decent discount will work well.

If you don't have your customers email address you can send a discount code attached to the invoice in their parcel. Don't make it seem too brash, simply say:

Thank you for ordering from my shop. To show my appreciation,
I've attached a x% discount code, which can be used towards
your next purchase.
Have a good day!

Newsletters are a way to keep customers informed of any new products you are selling. You can send them out monthly to keep your customers up to date with your shop. Offering helpful advice via articles can also help to keep someone interested in your business.

Discounts For Multiple Purchases

Etsy allow an automatic message to be sent after sales. You can also do this on your own website. Offering a buyer a discount to encourage them to buy again is a way to get someone to revisit your shop.

Freebies

There are three ways to offer freebies. The first is to offer a small sample of another product in your parcels. Try to have a few different samples to offer customers to tempt them to try your other products. This works well with items such as candles. I have bought from several shops who offer samples as melts and I often then go and buy a full-size version.

The second is to offer a competition. This works really well on social media where you share posts and get a large amount of traffic. Adding an extra discount code for people who participate also will encourage sales.

Thirdly, consider collaborating with someone. Both parties combine products and either run a competition or agree to share business cards. Make sure you are both appealing to the same sort of customer or this won't be worth your time.

Helpful Information

Writing blog posts is a great way to get your site to be considered more trustworthy. Producing relevant, helpful and most importantly shareable information, means that more people will visit your site. Some examples would be:

- Candle makers: make posts for common candle problems and how to fix them.
- Sewing: how to fix common machine issues or how to do an 'x' stitch.
- Jewellery: how to use two materials together or ways to use silver and gold.
- If you do build up enough helpful material, consider creating a course.

26

Writing Product Descriptions That Sell

A product description states what the product is and why you should buy it. As well as giving the customer key information, the point to a product description is to persuade someone to buy the item.

While it sounds easy, it can be challenging for someone who has never written one before. While customers are interested in your product details, they also want to know why they should buy your item as opposed to the same item in another shop. There are several elements to consider when writing a description:

Focus on a Problem Your Customer Has

This works well for practical items, you ask a question and they answer it:

Are you fed up with the amount of plastic you use in your daily life? Are you looking for ways to reduce this? Using cloth menstrual pads during your period can prevent an estimate d ten plastic backed pads from ending up in a landfill site. Our £7.99 cloth based pads are made from recyclable materials and last for an

average of two years. That means you'll save 240 pieces of plastic
from ending up in a landfill site.

In this example, the buyer is eco conscious. I've helped with the problem of reducing plastic waste in her life by providing a viable alternative at a reasonable cost.

Turn Mundane Details Into Benefits.

You might think using natural ingredients in soap is good. Your customer might not. I could write about soap and not include the benefits of using organic ingredients. Or I could write about using natural ingredients and all the benefits they bring to the buyer.

At the Soap Makers, we source natural ingredients to use in our
soap. Natural ingredients are known to be more suited to delicate
skin types as well as being better for the planet. Our Oat soap uses
organically grown oats and organic goat milk to make a natural
soap that is not only good for sensitive skin but also smells divine.

The benefits of using natural ingredients: suitable for sensitive skin and good for the environment.

Focus On the Technical Details

Just telling a customer your product is great with no detail as to why is at best met with eye rolls, or at worst, the customer doesn't buy from you. You don't have to say you're the best, you need to try to show it.

All our sewing bags are hand stitched for extra durability. We use
genuine leather in all of our bags to ensure they are hard wearing
and long lasting.

I've focused on durability and the hardiness of the bags. To really push sales, I'd advise looking at your competitors again and see what they focus on. This could be the quality of material used, the handmade nature of the items or even just prompt shipping? Focusing on quality is always a good way to entice a customer as no one wants to spend money on something they need to replace after a short time.

Use Reviews

Had a brilliant review from a customer? Why not include it in your description? I'd always ask a customer first and make sure you protect their identify by using their first name only. What better way of endorsing your product is there than by someone who has used it?

Sell a Tale

Selling online is harder than selling in person. You are asking a lot of a customer by trying to get them to buy a product they can see but not touch or use before parting with their money. Making you seem like a real person and someone they would want to buy from can improve your chances.

Ever since I first watched the Harry Potter films, I desperately wanted my own version of Hedwig. I begged my mum and then my dad who both agreed, an owl was not an acceptable pet. They both suggested I turn my hand to make one myself. So, I turned my hand to making my own version, in wool. After many failed attempts using other people's very expensive patterns, I decided to make my own. My first attempt is still sitting on my bookcase and I am so proud of it. I realised how frustrating it is for beginners to use patterns when wanting to attempt bigger products, so I've used my knowledge to design easy to make, simple knitting patterns for complete beginners. I want every knitter to feel the pride I did when I first made my Hedwig.

Through this you learn about the motivation of the seller to make their product as well as a little bit about the seller. This is useful to remove barriers between you and your customers.

Look at Reviews

Looking at the customer reviews of products will help you fine tune your descriptions. If someone mentions a competitor's candles don't last long, you should make sure yours do and put emphasis on how long they do last.

If they say a hand sewn make up bag feels cheap, make sure you focus on how durable it is. Focus on the language used in these reviews. if an item is commonly referred to by a different name, use that in your descriptions too to help buyers find your product.

Sense Inciting Words

These are words that describe using the senses to illicit an emotional response. Smooth and rich chocolate sounds better than milk chocolate. Bright and bold patterns sound better than novelty patterns. You can brainstorm ideas by looking at emotional language used to describe similar products. Focus on one or two senses that are relevant. A knitter won't care about how the wool smells, but a buyer of soap will.

Layout

No one has the time to read a page long product

description. Punctuate key features with bullet points and use short paragraphs to make it easy to read. You can write in sensible paragraphs, but remember people want to be able to read the key bits of information quickly. So use short paragraphs to persuade people to buy your product (sense inducing words) and the bullet points to get key messages across.

Writing descriptions takes practice. Big companies will have a team of copy writers to do the work for them, while you are reliant on yourself. However, this can be an advantage as no one is as passionate about your products as you. So go out there and tell everyone why your product is so great and why they should buy one.

27

Workbook: Part Five

Lesson One

- What are the key words someone would use to find your product? Google AdWords can help but so can searching on a search engine or within Etsy. i.e. 'Necklace'
- What are the common search terms for your product? Google Trends can help for less niche products such as candles. i.e. ' Organic Candles'
- Search for your competitors online. What key words/common search terms did you type in to find them?
- Are there any words you could use yourself to describe your products?
- What keywords could you use in your title (Heading One)?
- What keywords could you use in your subtitle (Heading Two)?

- What keywords could you use in text (Heading Three)?
- What social media links could you use?
- How could you have other websites link to you?

Lesson Two

- Which two social media sites would you focus on and why?
- Look at your competitors. How do they interact with their customers?
- What ways could you promote to customers that is individual to your item?
- Design a simple image based advert. Limit this advert to three lines of text and draw a picture of the sort of photograph you would include.
- Using your ideal customer list from Chapter Two, who might you target your adverts to? Think about age range, sex, hobbies, behaviour on and offline as well as location.

Lesson Three

- If you were a customer, what sort of questions do you think you would like to know about your product? Ask family and friends to help you if you can for extra support.
- How would you answer these questions?
- Can you think of any negative questions a customer might ask ?
- How would you turn that question around to show your product in a positive light?

- What are your worries when it comes to selling in person at places such are fairs?
- How can you turn these into Positive Learning Experiences?
- Do you know of any local events have happen regularly near you?

Fair Notes

- What items of stock will you take? How many of each type of stock will you take?
- Which payment method will you use?
- Which layout will you use to display your goods?
- What props will you take with you?
- What task could you take with you to look engaging and business like?
- What packaging will you take with you? Will you provide bags?
- Will you offer only one type of packaging or several such as gift wrapping?

Lesson Four

Newsletter

- What offer could you use to invite customers to sign up to your newsletter?
- What helpful industry information could you include?
- What other discount codes could you offer?
- What ways could you give freebies to customers?

- Could you collaborate with other sellers? Who could you work with?
- What free information could you give out on your website ?

Lesson Five

- What is your customers' main problem and what is the solution you offer to them?
- What are the 'mundane' details of your product? Think weight, size and ingredients.
- How can you turn these into benefits ?
- Why is your product the best on the market?
- At this stage, you might have reviews on your products. What key phases from the review below would you use in your description to help sell a product and why ? Why would you not include the whole review?

This is seriously the best product ever! The quality is great and I am so surprised it hasn't broken yet. For the price I think it's not bad and would buy again.

- Is there a mini tale you could tell in your description? Did you find a solution to your own problems with your product and think that the product might help others?
- What sensory words can be used in to describe your products?
- Looking at your competitors reviews, what key complaints are mentioned in their reviews?
- How can you turn them into benefits for your product?
- Example: *If your competitor has complaints about the*

shipping time, make sure you ship quicker and make a big deal of this in your descriptions.

- Using bullet points are important as well as small paragraphs. Have a go at writing a description using both bullet points and short paragraphs. Remember that you want your key points in bullet points as it will be the first thing you customer sees when they click on your link.

End of Chapter Questions

- Which three parts of this chapter have been the most helpful to you?
- Choose one thing from this chapter that you could use and implement today. What have you chosen and how are you going to implement it?

PART VI

Systems for Running Your Business

28

Dealing With Orders

To make things as easy as possible for yourself, you'll need to develop several systems to make the best use of your time.

Making items

- This will probably be your most time consuming task. There are ways to speed this up.
- Print all orders and have a tray to put them in, regularly check this tray (at least daily) for urgent orders
- Stock checking: once a week, do a quick stock check and order supplies promptly. Keep a sheet with your stock on it and regularly check off items when you need them.
- Part make orders: make as much in advance as you can. I make all my necklaces in one go and have pots for each variety. it takes around two hours from start to finish (done over several

days) to make and pack. But this saves me hours over the week. This tip is a lifesaver for someone with limited time.

Other suggestions:

- Candles: Wax the wicks (or buy wicks that are already waxed), stick wicks in jars and print labels off ready.
- Jewellery: put jump rings on chains or pendants and ready package items.
- Sewing: put needles with thread and cut shapes to correct size.

Even just getting labels ready for parcels will save you time. Stick some music on and make it a fun task.

Pack and Post

Having a clear postal schedule on your selling platform will allow you to be more flexible with postal times. You don't need to go to the post office every day, but you will need to go several times a week. I go three to four times a week with several orders. If I have an urgent order, I will make a special trip, but I charge extra for that service.

Have a small packing station. I bought a plastic case that I store all of my packing materials inside of it.

Establishing what you need for your packaging station and keeping it regularly topped up saves time. I keep:

- Scissors
- Tape
- Gift tags and ribbon
- Pillow boxes
- Velvet bags

- Bubble wrap
- Labels
- Return labels
- Brand labels
- Envelopes

Have a system to store pre-made items. as I said earlier, I use two boxes. If you stock more, consider shelving units or even a moving trolley. As long as it is kept away from children or pets, then use whatever works for you. Pinterest has creative suggestions for you to use and adapt if you search for office storage.

Regularly check how you can keep postage costs low. If you post a significant number of parcels, then check if your post office offers discounts. Check every few months as schemes change.

Recording sales

No matter how small your business is, you need a system to keep track of your sales. Having a quick way to find out how much you have made will also help you monitor your business.

When orders come in on Etsy, you'll be able to see your orders section. I fulfil my orders by copying the addresses on to labels by handwriting them. I don't need to store addresses for monitoring purposes. Etsy allow you to export data under Finances-Payment Account. You can click each month and download all the purchase orders from each month. All I use in my accounts (for tax) is the order ID and the amount I receive (Including postage). I used to track my sales before Etsy took its fees, but they now take them at source, so I don't need to.

If you have your own website, you'll have to compile this data yourself. You'll need to decide whether to record each sale in a spreadsheet or in an order book. Before I found that I could export order information, I kept a spreadsheet where I wrote down the order once I received it and would then put an asterisk in the last column to tell me it had been posted. Saves you sending an order twice.

Recording expenses

Once a month, I write down all the places I have bought from, the dates, the amount and then the item name. This is the beginning of my tax system. I input my postage from receipts in a separate colour with the date and amount. If you have other in person purchases, then be sure to record those too.

You can either use a digital system where you take photos of receipts once you've put them in your expenses area or use a physical system. I keep all of mine in a folder and include sections for each month. I then put the corresponding receipts in each area.

It takes me fifteen minutes to do my monthly orders and expenses which means it to only takes an additional half an hour at the end of each tax year. Time well spent. Include all business related expenses as this is important for tax purposes.

29

Tax Record System

Gross vs Net Profit

When running even a small business, you need to keep accurate records for tax purposes. You may not earn a huge amount initially, but you will still need to complete a Self-Assessment Tax form as an individual. The two basic pieces of information you need to record are income from sales and expenses you've incurred.

Completing a SE form is not that complicated but if you are worried about it, you'll need to hire someone to complete them for you. If you hire someone, they tell you how they want the information presented to them.

Your gross income is income before expenses. If you sold one necklace at £100, that's your gross profit. If you wanted to know what your profit was once you've taken all your expenses out of the equation (your net profit) then you would so a simple calculation:

Gross profit- expenses = Net Profit

It is a good idea to know both your gross and net profit so that you can see if you can make savings to increase how much you make.

Expenses

All business will have expenses. It is essential you find a way to record them. You need a system that allows for physical purchases that may have paper receipts and digital purchases.

My Personal System

• A File With Poly Pockets: Each has a sticker with a month for each tax year. I put all postage receipts and receipts from physical purchases each month.

• Spreadsheet: Each month, I record expenses on one side and orders on the other. For my expenses, I include the date, place, item and price. I would put postage here too. Across the sheet, and I usually leave a space of several columns so it's less confusing, I put my orders in there. Now that Etsy takes their fees out directly, make sure you select Etsy's 'Order Net'. This means it will show you what you have left after Etsy has removed their fee. As you need to remove your own expenses, this becomes your 'Order Gross'.

• An example:

Date	Place	Item	Price	Order ID	Order Gross
10/11/18	eBay	Backs	5.00	123456	17.98
12/11/18	Royal mail	Postage	2.50	1234567	14.99

Allowable expenses

When you are self-employed, you can deduct certain running costs for your business to pay less tax. These are called 'allowable expenses'.

If you have a business that makes £5000 profit a year but £1000 expenses, you would pay tax on £4000 as long as all of your expenses where allowable.

Allowable expenses examples:

Banking

- Bank overdrafts, credit card charges and interest on bank and business loans.
- Hire purchase, interest and leasing payments.
- Insurance for business.

Reselling Goods

- Stock
- Raw materials (elements you use to make your products)

Marketing, Entertainment and Subscriptions

- Advertising in newspapers
- Mailshots
- Website costs
- Free samples
- Trade/professional journals
- Membership to organisations if related to your business.

Office Equipment

- Bills: mobile, phone and internet
- Business postage (not for posting orders to customers)
- Stationary
- Printing/ink

- Computer software for business

Do seek legal and financial advice if you are in doubt as to what counts. For the UK, you can find more information at: www.Gov.uk/expenses-if-your-self-employed .

Reinvesting/saving

It's always good practice to keep some cash in reserve in case of increases in orders and you need to buy more stock. I always aim to keep £100 in the account. I also deduct 10% to put into business savings so should I want to reinvest in equipment I can. I also save 20% of profits in my savings too to cover my tax/ national insurance bill. If you owe less, then you can either play voluntary contributions to make sure you are still entitled to a pension or just keep it as savings.

30

Terms and Conditions

It doesn't matter if you sell on your own website or on Etsy, when it comes to online selling, you'll need terms and conditions. If you sell on Etsy, they have their own set rules you must follow and are allowed to put into your own terms. Your terms can't go against Etsy's. More information can be found at www.etsy.com/legal .

Delivery

Basic things such as your processing time (the time it takes you to make and are ready to ship) as well as estimated delivery times will also be necessary. It is always worth checking your country's post office website to see what they estimate for each country and its own terms. Royal Mail for example, expect you to wait thirty working days before raising a complaint of a lost parcel.

Payment

If you are selling on Etsy, they will have a variety of acceptable payment methods for you to choose from. You don't need accounts with these companies in order to get money from them as Etsy handles all of that. On your own website, you need to decide how you will accept payment. Using a recognised brand such as PayPal will install trust in your business.

Returns, Exchanges and Cancellations

Firstly, you need to decide if you accept returns or exchanges. EU residents have extra protection. They have 14 days to return goods after receiving them. They can return for any reason in this time period. As a seller, you must return the original postage costs and the original cost of the item. The buyer must ship the item back to you at their own cost which you do not have to return. Make sure your buyer returns via a trackable method so you can verify you have received it. This doesn't include perishable goods or made to order goods.

Your policy must clearly state these rights, or your buyers' rights are extended to a year in which they can return. You should also have a line to explain your cancellation policy, including how much notice should they give you to return.

Privacy policy

If you are in the EU, this is essential, whether you sell on Etsy or your own site. It's your way of showing a buyer how you will use their data and how they can opt out or request their own information. This will be covered in the GDPR chapter.

Returns procedure

I would advise having an email already prepared. Have

the buyer first write to you so that they can request a return. You need to request information such as the order number and the buyers address as well as the item. An example would be:

Thank you for contacting me and I am sorry to hear that you would like to return your item. If you could please send me your order number, address and the name of the item you ordered, I will be happy to help.

Once they have responded, I would send the following message:

Thank you for providing that information. In order to process your return, you will need to return the item to me at the following address…

Please include a note with your order number and address on it.

Once I have received your item, I will process your return. Please note that the item must be in sellable condition. You will receive your original payment back along with your original delivery costs. You must return the item at your own expense and this element will not be refunded.

Refunds will be processed within 7-10 days.

Make sure you handle all returns promptly in order to be fair to your buyer.

31

Business Banking

Most banks, even if you are self-employed, will expect you to use a paid business account. The fees vary from a set monthly amount to a charge per transaction, cheque or deposit.

There will be more in-depth checks carried out when you open up a business bank account. Each year, you will be expected to complete a short form detailing how you make money and how it is invested. It only takes twenty minutes and you will also be expected to produce evidence that you still live at the same address.

Finding a business bank account shouldn't be a hardship. High street banks usually offer some form of banking to businesses. The easiest route to obtaining a business bank account is from the bank you do your own personal banking with. This isn't always the cheapest way, but it is the easiest.

To find the best business account, spend time researching which bank Is best for you and your business. I made the following form:

	Charge per month	Incentive to join	Special accounts for small businesses	Charges for transactions
Bank 1	5.00	18 months free	Yes- an online only business account	50p per £100 deposited if I paid in more than £3000. 40p per cheque 40p to withdraw in branch
Bank 2	7.50	18 months free	Yes, start-ups only.	70p charge if depositing over £1000

You might have different criteria depending on whether you sell on a stall as well as online. But find an account that would suit you for most transactions. You can move your account if the banks terms and conditions allow you to after a certain period. It can be a pain, but it means you can take advantage of the free offers.

32

How to Handle Complaints and Returns

How you handle things when something goes wrong will show your professionalism to a customer. Even if something goes horribly wrong, handling it well means you have a higher chance of your customer coming back.

Returns

Even if you sell on Etsy as opposed to your own website, you are an independent seller. Etsy does not tell you how to handle returns; that's up to you. Having a generic returns form will help you to handle your returns quickly and efficiently. Rules of returns:

- Be polite at all times.
- Don't try to dissuade someone from returning an item. You can offer a discount if they would rather keep the item (and you don't want the hassle of having to deal with a return , but don't be difficult.
- Refund your customers promptly.
- Treat customers as you'd like to be treated.

- Have clear polices and stick to them. Make sure they are easy to understand and easy to find.

How someone sends you the return is up to you. In the EU, you must provide a cancellation form, but the buyer doesn't need to use it to return. I have never had anyone use one. You should include the following on your cancellation form:

- Date ordered
- Item name
- Order number
- Reason for return
- Statement to the effect of "I wish to cancel my order."
- Address, contact details and name of customer
- Address, contact details and name of business

To keep things simple, you can have the same polices for everyone. I use this method so that even people who are outside of the EU have the same shopping experience. It also saves me time having to check where the buyer is from.

Complaints

No one likes to receive a complaint, but it is a part of running a business. Too many complaints can ruin a business. This is why it is essential to handle all complaints with dignity.

. . .

Common Complaints and Solutions:

Delay That Isn't Your Fault.

- Problem: A customer orders an item and it turns up after your estimated delivery time. It still arrives before the thirty working day deadline. The customer is upset as it was a gift.
- Solution: The first thing you should do is apologise. Even if it isn't your fault, sometimes people just want their problem to be acknowledged. Second, point out in you polices, highlighting that the delivery time frames are only estimates. Apologise, again, if the policy was not clear enough.
- Example:

'Hi (customer name), I am so sorry that your item did not arrive in time for your friend's birthday. I know how frustrating it is when a gift does not turn up due to mail delay. I shipped the item fifteen days ago (23/06/19) and so it should have arrived on time. As you can see in my polices, I list delivery times as estimates rather than guarantees. I apologise if this was not displayed clearly enough. The large majority of my items arrive well before these estimates, but due to external issues, sometimes this does not happen. I do hope your friends had a nice birthday and that they liked their present. Have a great day!

Delay That is Your Fault

- Problem: A customer makes an order and you misplace it. They still haven't got their item.

- Solution: You need to be honest, but not overly candid. Explain that you misplaced it, but you are now sending it out urgently. If you can, send it via the quickest postal service you can find, at your own cost. Also offer the buyer the chance to cancel the purchase if they would rather.
- Example:

Hi (Customer name),I am so sorry you item has not arrived yet. Due to a processing error, your order was not dispatched with the other orders of that day. I appreciate this is not the service you would expect from me. I can either offer you a full refund or, if you will allow me, I will post your order today and get it shipped in a fast-tracked postal method at no cost to yourself. It should arrive to you within three working days. I'd also like to refund your postage costs as a further apology. If you would kindly reply to this message, telling me which option you would prefer, I will happily do either as quickly as I can . Once again, sorry for the inconvenience, Kind regards.

Item Arrives Broken

- Problem: Item arrives damaged. Customer is very annoyed.
- Solution: You have two options: refund or replace. Ideally, you would replace and give some money back for the postage. If your material costs are high, then this might not be an option as it would cost you a significant amount of money to lose two pieces.
- Example:

Hi (customer name),I am sorry to hear that your item arrived broken. I make sure all my items are carefully wrapped to avoid damage but sometimes this is inevitable. I am happy to either offer a replacement item or a full refund. If you would let me know which option you would prefer, I will deal with your issue quickly. Kind regards.

You can offer discount codes, free shipping or free expedited shipping in the event of something going wrong. What you offer will depend on your margins. Huge companies tend to offer replacements and money off postage rather than deal with a return as it costs them time and money. Customers are also far more likely to come back if they are happy.

33

Monitoring Your Business

When running a business, it is important to keep records so you can evaluate its progress. You might want to know how well adverts are performing or what stock sells best. To check this, big businesses do regular small audits and a comprehensive one once a year. It is up to you how often you do it. If you are going to do one annually, try to make sure you do it on either the same date or as close to this as possible. Trying to monitor your business in summer after doing a major audit in winter will mean you could get distorted results.

Goals and Checklists

One way to regularly monitor yourself is to set up regular goals or have a check list. Some people might set monthly goals. Others may operate a checklist system that is completed over the course of a year.

You can break down larger tasks into smaller sub-tasks in order to complete a large goal.

SMART Goals

If you want to make your goals more achievable, consider using a SMART goal setting system.

Goal 1: Set Up Webpage with Five Listings By the End of the Month.

♣ Specific: Are they clear and defined?

♣ Measurable: How can you decided if the goal is completed? What will you use to measure how completed the goal is?

♣ Attainable: Is the goal realistic?

♣ Relevant: Is it an important goal for your business?

♣ Time based: Have you included when you need to have completed the task?

Monthly Task Breakdown

Break down your goal into smaller tasks once you have set your SMART goal.

o Month One: Set Up Website with Five Listings By the End of the Month.

♣ Buy domain name (week1)

♣ Find hosting (week1)

♣ Find and install theme (week 2)

♣ Add written content (week 2)

♣ Add shop element (week 3)

♣ List five items in shop (week 3)

♣ Set up payment system (week 4)

♣ Do trial purchase (week 4)

♣ You can do this monthly if weekly is too much or even every quarter.

Types of Reviews

Once you've set goals, you will want to find ways of checking you are reaching them.

Financial Reviews

You want to see how much money you make per year in this section. Questions you might ask yourself are:

♣ Which item was a best seller?

♣ How can I reduce costs to make more profit?

♣ Which adverts worked well? Why?

♣ Is it possible to increase the sales price?

♣ How much did I make as profit?

You might want to break this down into a monthly task. I keep records for tax purposes on a monthly basis. This means I can work out how effectively things like adverts are working for me, as I can look at my sales before, during and after the advert runs. I can also see what the trends are for each time of the year. I know November and December are very busy for me.

On Etsy you can track your adverts on their dashboard. It even tells you how much each advert generated in spending which is helpful.

Online Reviews

If you use social media, you might want to know:

- How many people follow you?
- Which posts get the most engagement?
- What is the average engagement per post?
- Which posts lead to a higher amount of sales?

You can then replicate this model for other posts. Don't churn out the same posts day in day out but find what works and use that more often. Working out your conversation rate (the amount of effort/money put in vs how much you get back) will help you decide if the effort you are making in certain fields is worth it.

Example: *I have 200 likes on an advert but only 15 sales. My conversion rate would be 15/200= 7.5% so, 7.5% of people buy my products after viewing that advert.*

Ways I can improve my conversion rate might include to experiment with different pictures or run sales/competitions. Its trial and error.

If you sell at markets, you would want to know similar things, such as:

- How much you made in person vs online?
- Which months are better for selling?
- What items are popular?
- Are they popular at certain times?

You don't have to count how many people visit your shop every time. But once in a while, do an informal tally of how many customers come to your stall. You can then work out your conversion rate. This will also tell you if certain times/ places are not worth selling at for the effort put in. Use the same time of year to compare; there is no point comparing Christmas with Easter.

Record system

Whatever data you collect, you need a way to easily store it and be able to compare it. Excel or a paper notebook will work well. You can either:

- Write questions and answer them.
- Input the data into a spreadsheet.

It depends if you want it to be numbers or word driven, which is a personal choice.

34

Wholesale

If you feel you can make money, wholesale can be a good opportunity for a business. It requires you to be able to make a large quantity of goods and sell them at a lower price than you would if you were selling to the public. You make money due to the large number of items you shift.

You have two options when it comes to wholesale:

Independent

These shops will take items from new sellers and will be willing to give you a go. They will most likely want to take only a few items initially to test the sales potential, as well as working on a sale or return basis. This means you get your money for your items only once they are sold by the shop. The shop can also return items it doesn't want without It costing them anything. It is important to research these shops to make sure you share similar customers.

. . .

Big stores

These companies have a set way of dealing with new items and it can take some time to hear back from them. They will usually take a large order (for you) to trial your product which can be at short notice. You will also need to make sure your items are suitable for their shop and follow their set standards. You may also have to wait several months for payments due to their accounting system. This is fine if it is a stable business, and you can afford to wait for payment, but if it is a large business and something goes wrong, you've lost a lot of money.

Prices for wholesale

- Cost x 2=wholesale
- Cost x3=your price if selling to a customer.

It is up to you what price you would like to accept and you need to be willing to negotiate terms so that both you and the shop/company get a fair deal. It will be easier to negotiate after they have had your product for several trials and seen they are selling well, rather than before they've tried them.

Tips

- Always have samples to show prospective businesses.
- Research shops. You need to make sure your items will fit in there.
- Be willing to accept your products may be used in sales/promotions.

- Make sure you can fulfil all orders before agreeing to them. If you let the business down, they are unlikely to use you again.

35

Workbook: Part Six

Lesson One

- What ways could you save time when it came to making your products?
- How could you keep a record of how much stock you have? How often would you update it?
- What items do you need in your postal/packing kit?
- How will you store your items?
- What system will you use to record sales?
- How could you record your expenses?
- What expenses would you record?
- In your notebook or in excel, design a sheet for keeping track of your orders and expenses .

Lesson Two

- What are the definitions of Gross profit and Net profit?
- How do you work out your Net Profit?
- What system will you use to store your tax information?
- What allowable expenses can you claim?
- What would be a sensible cash flow amount to keep in your business account each month?

Lesson Three

You can use the questions here as prompts for writing your own policy.

Delivery

- How long will it take you to make and post your orders?
- What are your estimated delivery times for the UK, Europe, USA, Australia and the rest of the world? Remember to add the maximum delivery time frame. In the UK, this is 30 days.
- Will you charge for priority shipping? How much will you charge?
- Will you charge extra to rush though an order? How much extra?

Payment

- What payment methods will you accept?

Returns, Cancellations and Exchanges

- For made to order items or perishables, will you accept returns?

- What is your returns procedure? (make sure you follow EU guidelines if you are in the EU).
- How many days do customers have to return items to your or contact you about a return?
- Who pays for return postage?
- How quickly will you refund?
- Can customers (outside of the EU) return for any reason?
- Do you require trackable return postage ?
- Who pays import taxes and fees?
- Will you accept cancelations?
- How much time do you need to accept cancelations?
- Will you accept exchanges?
- Who pays postage?

Privacy Policy

- How will you store personal information? If you don't see personal information such as payment information as its handled by a third party, include this in your policy.
- Who has access to customers personal information?
- Who should be contacted in case of problem or wanting to see personal data?
- What data do you collect?
- Why do you need this data and how will you use it?
- How long do you keep this data?
- How will you display the Rights of the user in your policy?
- Who should be contacted in case of problem or wanting to see personal data as well as general enquires?

Lesson Four

- Choose four bank accounts to compare. For each account, find out the following:
- What are the charges per month?
- Do they have Incentives to join the bank?
- Do they have Special accounts?
- What are there charges for transactions?

Lesson Five

- Will you keep the same policy for the EU as for elsewhere?
- On what occasion might you be flexible with your polices?
- What complains might you have?
- Choose one complaint you think you might receive. Write a draft email to the customer to assist them with their complaint.
- What ways can you appease unhappy customers?

Lesson Six

SMART Goals

- Choose a goal you want to achieve in your business. Write the goal in your note book making sure it is SMART.

Monthly Goals

- Using your SMART goal, break it down into

smaller tasks to be completed in the next
month.

Financial Review

- What questions might you want to know in
  your financial review?

- Would you conduct a review monthly or yearly?

Online/In-Person Review

- How regularly would you track your online
  presence?
- If an advert had 300 views, and 24 sales, what
  is the conversion?
- *Answer: 24/300 = 12/150 = 4/50 x2 =8/100
  or 8%*
- If you have a stall, what days might you
  compare? Why?
- What system would you use to record your
  online review?

Lesson Seven

- What items do you have that would sell well
  wholesale?
- Which businesses could you approach to sell
  them for you?
- Why would these businesses be a good fit for
  your brand?
- What are the pros and cons of dealing with an
  independent shop?

- What are the pros and cons of dealing with a large company?

End of Chapter Questions

- Which three parts of this chapter have been the most helpful to you?
- Choose one thing from this chapter that you could use and implement today. What have you chosen and how are you going to implement it?

PART VII

Legal Stuff

36

Self-Employed vs Setting Up a Company

When running a small business, you have two ways of registering; you can either be a sole trader or set up a limited company. Both have their benefits and costs. It is up to you to decide what is appropriate for your business.

The Upsides of Registering as Sole Trader

Making the leap from being employed to being a sole trader tends to be easier for people to manage than changing from employed to running a company. Becoming a sole trader is as simple as letting HMRC know (via an online form) that you are a sole trader. This can be completed in under an hour. You can start trading immediately. Your accounts will be easy to manage – you just declare what you have earned via a self-assessment form once a year. If your bank allows you to, you can also run your business from a current account rather than paying for a business bank account, which saves on fees.

The Downsides of Registering as a Sole Trader

The perception of dealing with a company can instil confidence in other businesses as well as customers. It shows you are serious. This is not impossible as a sole trader, but you will need to work harder to achieve this perception of professionalism. The other downside is that the risks are all yours. If you don't have insurance and someone is injured by your product (and then they sue you), you are personally responsible. This means your own money and possessions can be used to pay a debt if you lose your legal case. As a company, you are not personally liable, instead it is the company and its assets that are at risk.

The Upsides of Registering as a Company

The positives of forming a company may not appear that great. But as a company, you will get better tax breaks when compared to a sole trader. You are able to take both a salary (at lower tax rate than a sole trader) and you also benefit from dividends as a shareholder of your company. The added protection you have should something go wrong is also appealing. If there are not enough assets to seize following a legal action, then the company is dissolved and there are no further penalties that can be imposed against you.

The Downsides of Registering as a Company

The process of setting up and running a company is vastly different from being a sole trader. You are responsible for far more paperwork and face large fines if it is completed incorrectly. You are also expected to have a business bank account which will come with fees so this needs to be budgeted into your accounts. As the accounting procedure required of a business is more complex than for a sole trader, it might be worth considering paying someone to do it for you.

As with any decisions related to your business, do make sure you thoroughly investigate your options and seek legal advice if in doubt.

37

How to Register a Company

Different countries will have different rules on setting up a company. If you locate the relevant government website, you will find key information on the rules and regulations for setting up a company. A public company floats shares on the stock market, a private company doesn't sell on the stock market but you can sell shares to existing stock holders.

In the UK, setting up a company is broken down into the following steps:

Choose a Name for Your Company
You will need to check if the name is trademarked. You will need to check if the name is available as you can't use the same name as an already established business.

Follow set rules on names of companies:

- Not similar to another company.
- Can't use the word 'accredited' unless the Department for Business, Energy and Industry gives you permission.

- Can't contain 'LTD' in title.

Choose a Director and Company Secretary

- You must have at least one director.
- Directors are legally responsible for the company and must make sure the company follows its legal obligations.
- They must have a UK registered address as this is displayed on Companies House.
- The sectary takes over some jobs from the director. You don't require a secretary for a private limited company. If you sell shares publicly, then you do.
- Not everyone can be a secretary or a director. They must be over eighteen and must not have been bankrupt (unless this is discharged as the debt has been cleared).

Choose Shareholders

- The majority of Ltd companies are owned by shareholders. These shareholders own the company and can vote on how the company is run. You are also entitled to dividends on the profits (a share of them) and this is taxable.
- All Ltd companies must have at least one shareholder. Even if it just the director of the company.
- If it's a private company and you give the shares away for free, they will have an associated value. If the company ceases trading,

the shareholder has to pay the value back to the company.

- You will need to keep a record of shareholders.

List Who Has Significant Control

- Anyone with over 25% of shares will need to be listed as a PSC (Person of Significant Control)

Complete Documents for How You Will Run the Company

You need to compile two documents.
Articles of association:

- Rules that govern your company.
- Who has shares, how often directors meet and what products the company trades in.?
- Examples of this can be found online.

Memorandum of association:

- A legal document signed by shareholders to agree to setting up the company.

Records

You need to inform Companies House if records are not kept at the registered company address.

Records to keep:

- Directors, secretary and shareholders information.
- Results of meetings and votes.
- Any payment promises.
- Information about when shares are bought and sold.
- PSC information. If they have over 25%

control, can remove or appoint directors or influence the company.

- Accounts information. Money spent and received, stock taking, debts and loans as well as assets of the company.

38

Registering as a Sole Trader

Registering as a sole trader is a far simpler process than registering as a company. The overall running of the business is also relatively easy; you just need to submit your self-assessment tax accounts to HMRC once a year.

Choose a Name to Trade Under

Some traders may trade under their own name while others want to use a different name to keep everything separate. There are a few names you can't use:

- Can't include 'LTD' in the title if not a company.
- Can't be rude or offensive.
- Can't be the name of an existing company or trademark.
- You can't use the word 'accredited' unless the Department for Business, Energy and Industry have granted you its use.

To check for trademarks: www.gov.uk/search-for-trademark

Know Which Records to Keep

You need to keep a simple accounting system which fundamentally displays any incoming and outgoing money. You can get an accountant to do it for you or do it yourself using a template. Once you are decided on how you are going to record your business information, set a regular date either weekly or monthly to input this into your system.

Any profit is then yours. This is your wage. It is a good idea to keep a record of what you pay yourself as this is taxable.

Register for Self-Assessment Tax

You need to register as self-employed within two years of trading. I registered immediately as I found this easier when keeping records.

You complete a quick form to get a ten-digit Unique Taxpayer Reference (UTR in the UK). This takes ten days to arrive. Once you have your reference you can complete your tax forms online or print them off and send them. It takes thirty to sixty minutes to complete a form. If you keep good records, this is simplified and so not a difficult task.

39

Specific Insurances

Regardless of what you manufacture, it is always a good idea to consider insurance. Freak accidents do happen. If you are working with anything that could easily hurt a person (i.e. candles), I would strongly recommend it.

There are two types of insurances you can look at:

Specific

These are insurance companies who know what the risks are of producing items like candles. They'll know the value of your equipment and the costs should something go wrong. They can also be a little more expensive than generic insurances and harder to find.

Example: Blackfriars Group

Generic

These companies cater for all types of business. It might include things you didn't think you needed as standard and other extras such as insurance for fairs. You can end up paying for things you don't need and are not relevant.

Examples: Direct line Craft Insurance and Craft Cover

Elements of Insurance to Consider

All insurance policies will offer different elements with some parts not being relevant to you. It is important for you to examine exactly what is included to be sure you are getting the cover you need.

- Legal Fee Cover: Should someone sue you or you need to sue them, your fees will be covered.
- Online Cover: Costs covered include loss of business from cyber-attacks. Some also include Ransomware cover.
- Public Liability Cover: This covers you if a member of the public is accidentally hurt by you or a staff member of your business.
- Product Liability Cover: This covers you if someone is injured or made ill by one of your products.
- Contents, Stock and Tools Cover: You will be covered should your equipment be damaged due to a fire, flood other natural disasters. You can also get cover that protects you when you are at a stall or at home.
- Business Disruption Cover: If your workspace is flooded or loses power, you will need somewhere else to work. Some policies will also protect you should a place you trade in (market or stall) have problems that affect you.
- Buildings Cover: If you have an outbuilding you work in, then this cover would be applicable to you. Check your home insurance

first to see if it would cover you for business use as this might be cheaper.

- Employers Liability Cover: This is only relevant if you employ someone. You will need this in case a staff member is injured during work. Even if someone does not work for you full time (even for just a few hours), then you can be liable should something go wrong.
- Theft Cover: Should someone steal from you and your business; you would be compensated.

Most home insurances will not cover your business. This means even if your house is flooded, your business equipment is not covered. For the sake of a few pounds a month, having additional cover is something worth looking into.

You can find insurances for your specific or generic needs via online search engines and comparisons sites. Simply type in the nature of the business your run and the word 'insurance' and you will see a variety of options.

40

Specific Legislation and Relevant Agencies

Not all categories of business require specific legislation, but the obligation is on you to check. If you don't, you can be handed a large fine and even have your business shut down.

Specific Legislation

Businesses that have risky practices will require you to adhere to legal regulations. Candles, wax melts and reed diffusers for example, require all labels to be Classification, Labelling and Packaging compliant (CLP). There are set things you must include on your packaging such as certain words or pictograms. If you don't, you face a large fine and your business insurance will be deemed invalid.

The painful part is that each label must be specific to the product, so you can't so a generic one and include for each scent. A lavender candle will have a different label to a peach candle.

It can be daunting but there is software that does the label making for you. Alternatively, you can buy from companies who provide data sheets so that you can copy information (such as ingredients) over to your label.

To check if your business has any specific legislation attached to it, do a simple search of ' your business type - legislation' and see what comes up. Trading standards and council websites are also informative places to check.

You can find more information about specific requirements by visiting the Gov.uk website here: https://www.gov.uk/browse/business

Informing Relevant Agencies

Most small business won't be obliged to do this. Food making will require you to inform your local council so that they can inspect your premises. www.food.gov.uk is helpful in this area.

If you work from home and have a specific space, i.e. a room or an outbuilding, that is solely used for your business, then you may have to pay business rates. If it has other uses such as a home office, then you are not liable. Check with your local council if you are in doubt.

Remember that the obligation is on you, as the business owner, to check if your are compliant. Large companies don't always look like they are complying (take a look at some well-known candle companies), but they have a huge legal team to defend them should something go wrong. You don't.

41

Trademarks

If you decide to trade under a business name, you might consider looking at getting it trademarked. This is the process of legally claiming the logo or business name as yours so that no one else can use it.

When you register a trademark, you are able to:

- Use legal action to stop someone using your trademark without permission.
- Use the registered symbol ('R') that warns other not to use the name.
- You can sell or license your brand
- If you register your trademark, check where it is registered. Usually you register for the country you live in, but you can register internationally as well.

You can't register:

- Anything offensive.
- Use words that describe your item. You can't trademark the word 'necklaces' if you sell necklaces.
- Misleading words. Don't say you are vegan if you aren't.
- Anything that isn't unique.

Before you go through the process of trademarking a business name, make sure you check your trademark isn't already registered. You can check by searching for your trademark here: www.gov.uk/search-for-trademark

You may notice that a version of your idea is being used. Ideally, you should use an idea where no one else has used it. This means you are less likely to have objections.

Classes

You will also need to know what class you want to register your trademark in. Classes come in two types:

- 1-34 is for goods.
- 35-45 is for services.

A class is where your trademark is active. So, if you sell candles, you would register in class four (candles and wicks for lighting). Your trademark is not covered in other classes. This means, in theory, someone could use your name to sell a different product in another class. You can of course object, but this can be costly. If you think you might sell in more than one class, register accordingly before you start to sell.

Within each class are terms. Class four (fuels and illuminations) has several terms which include lubricants and electrical energy in addition to candles. You can include all of these terms in your application but its best to be specific.

You can check class types here: www.euipo.europa.eu/ec2

Costs

You have two options when it comes to cost.

1. Right start application. You pay £100 upfront and your application is then checked. You get a report saying if there are any potential objectors. If there aren't (or you don't feel they are close enough to your brand), then you pay an additional £100 and the application goes ahead.
2. Standard application. You pay £170 up front. This does not include a check and the application goes straight to the processing stage.

If you want to add extra classes, it is £50 per class. It is best to wait to get the first trademark agreed before pursuing additional classes.

The Process

1. Apply for the trademark. www.trademarksipo.gov.uk/ipo-apply
2. Wait to hear back (within twenty days) to

confirm everything is fine or for amendments to be requested.

3. If everything is fine, you have to wait for two months before the trademark is registered. During this time, your application will be lodged in the trademarks journal. Anyone can object to your trademark within this time. A further month is added to allow for this to be dealt with.

4. If no one objects, you are registered. You can now object should someone register a trademark similar to yours. You will need to renew the trademark every ten years so make sure your details are up to date.

42

GDPR

GDPR stands for General Data Protection. If you run a business, you will at some point come into contact with customers data. GDPR came into force in order to specify how data should be used and how it has to be protected. It replaces the Data Protection Act.

The Important Details of GDPR:

- Consent. You now need to prove you gained consent to obtain a customer's data. You also need to make sure customers are aware that they can withdraw this permission and how to do it.
- Breach notification. You have seventy-two hours to let customers know that they have been involved in a data breach.
- Right to access. Data Subjects (the customers whose data you hold) have the right to see what you hold on them for free. There needs to be a

Data Controller in your business who will deal with data. This is most likely you.

- Right to be forgotten. If the data is out of date, then the Data Subject has the right to ask for their data to be removed from your files.
- Data portability. Data Subjects can obtain and reuse their data for their own purposes. This can be between different computing environments.
- Privacy by design. Anyone who holds data should have systems designed for the protection of that data.
- Data protection officers. Qualified data protection officers should be employed in business or organisations where there are more than two hundred and fifty employees. Their roles are to maintain and process personal data.

A fine of up to 4% of the turnover of a business can be enforced if you don't comply.

It may cost you money to set up a GDPR compliant system, but it is a legal requirement. You can find out more information on this at : www.ico.org.uk/for-organisations/guide-to-data-protection .

There is also information for sole traders at : www.ico.org.uk/for-organisations/data-protection-self-assessment-for-small-businesses-and-sole-traders .

43

Workbook: Part Seven

Lesson One

- What are the pros and cons of setting yourself up as a Self-employed person?
- What are the pros and cons of registering yourself as a company?

Lesson Two

- Where would you find country specific information on registering your business?
- Have you checked if your company name is trademarked?
- Have you checked if your company name is similar to other names ?
- Have you checked that it doesn't go against rules for names of companies?
- Who is your director?
- Who is your secretary?

- What is the role of the director in your business?
- What is the role of secretary in your business?
- Who will be your shareholders?
- How much of a share will they get and how much is its worth?
- Who is a person who has significant control?
- Where will you find an example of articles of association?
- Where will you find an example of a memorandum of association?
- Where will you keep your records?
- How long should you keep records for?
- What government websites will be useful in setting up your business?

Lesson Three

- Have you checked if your business name is included in another company's name?
- Have you checked if your business name is offensive?
- Have you checked if your business name infringes on an existing trademark?
- Have you checked if your business name is linked to a government organisation?
- Have you found a simple accounting system you can use? (Etsy and Microsoft have some examples)
- Would you hire an accountant?
- What is your UTR number ? Have you kept it in a safe place?
- Will you fill in your forms online or on paper?

(Remember that paper forms tend to have an earlier deadline than online forms).

Lesson Four

- Which type of insurance would suit your business the most; generic or specific Insurance?
- Which elements of insurance do you think you need for your business?
- Using the internet, research three insurance companies that suit your needs and budget. What are the pros and cons of each?

Lesson Five

- What keywords will you use to search for key legislation?
- What information does your local council or trading standards provide?
- Do you need to adhere to specific legislation?
- What do you legally need to do to sell your products?
- Do you need to inform the local council that you have set up a business?
- Do you use a set room or outbuilding specifically for your business?
- Have you checked if you need to pay business rates?

Lesson Six

- Have you searched for your brand name and checked that it isn't trademarked?
- If the name is trademarked but you want to use it, how could you adapt the name so that it isn't going to infringe trademark laws?
- What classes could you register your trademark in?
- Which class fits your brand the most?
- Will you go with a Right Start or Standard application ?

Lesson Seven

- How will GDPR affect you as a business?
- How will you handle data in a protective way?
- If you completed the ICO Self-Assessment Form, how could you improve your handling of data?

End of Chapter Questions

- Which three parts of this chapter have been the most helpful to you?
- Choose one thing from this chapter that you could use and implement today. What have you chosen and how are you going to implement it?

PART VIII

Case Studies

44

Sally

Sally is married with two children under five. She knows she wants to sell eco-friendly candles, as she enjoys making them as gifts and thinks she could make a profit. Sally and her husband can't afford to live on one salary so Sally would need to earn at least £700 a month.

Chapter One - Sally

Sally would like more flexibility in her life as well as being in charge of her earning potential. With two children, Sally needs to be able to break tasks into smaller elements and be flexible in when she completes them.

She knows that there are downsides to candle making. The main issue is the amount of space the equipment requires and the cost to buy it all. However, the upside is that Sally doesn't need to spend the time or money learning a skill as she already knows how to make candles.

After sitting down with her husband, Sally finds they can make economies of around £300 a month. Sally will meal plan as well as shop in a cheaper supermarket. Her husband agrees to get a monthly travel card instead of a weekly one and take packed lunches to work. By using a comparison site, Sally and her husband saved £175 on their utilities. Sally now only needs to earn around £400 a month due to making these savings.

Sally has worked out a budget for what she needs. As she already owns moulds, she has saved herself money. But she still needs:

- Wax £32
- Fragrances £58.36
- Jars £21.21
- Boxes to pack £15.60
- Boxes to ship £13.00
- Safety labels £0.96
- Wicks £2.40
- Measuring jugs £5
- Labels £5.00
- Total: £153.53

Sally still has some maternity money left so she is going to use this to pay her initial start-up costs. She isn't going to use a website yet but will focus on Etsy and in-person selling.

She thinks her biggest problem will be not putting a product out until it is perfect. She has decided to make the leap and once she is happy with the product, she will release it. She knows she can go back and perfect the item later.

Sally is already a part of several Facebook groups for candle making. She brainstorms some keywords to search such as 'Candle Business' and 'Candle Makers' to find niche groups to join. She asks questions about label designers and where to find them. In return Sally answers a question someone asked about wick sizes.

She looks at her local councils' website and decides to email an enquiry about a space at the annual trade fair.

Chapter Two-Sally

Sally decides to go through the exercises even though she knows she wants to make and sell candles. She thinks she could sell her unique blend recipes later on to make passive income but wants to focus on making candles for now. After several attempts to narrow her field down, she decides to make eco-friendly candles from essential oils to be as natural as possible. Sally will investigate natural waxes she could use too.

She looks at the suggestions and finds Etsy and Instagram the most helpful. After comparing several products, she finds that most people want more environmentally sustainable candles so Sally will focus on this. Her ideal customers are eco-conscious women aged 18-50 who don't mind the cost of the product as long as it fits into their lifestyle morals. Her three USP's would be: High-end packaging that is recyclable, using eco-friendly wax and scenting her candles with essential oils. Her tag line would be: 'Luxury Eco-Friendly Candles Made with Natural Essential Oils.'

Sally has completed parts of her business plan. She has also added some notes on specific legislation that she will investigate later. She has done more research on the companies she will be competing with. She feels she can compete on customer service by replying quicker to customers as well as using higher quality ingredients. Sally will get into a habit of filling in a little more of her business plan at the end of each chapter in the book.

After narrowing down keywords, Sally has used a few websites to get stock. She has mostly used independent companies for fragrances and wax but larger companies for packing materials as this worked out cheaper.

She decides to go with Method Three as she wants at least £10 profit per candle. She can make twelve candles an hour which means her hourly rate would be £120.

After comparing options, Sally decides to use her USP's as inspiration for her business name 'Sally Jones - Luxury Candles'.

Chapter Three-Sally

Sally's back story is that she used to make candles with her grandmother who taught her to use natural ingredients in her candles. Using these methods, Sally can make natural and more eco-friendly candles.

She designs her logo on her computer using a logo generator. She decides to include her USP's underneath 'Luxury. Eco-friendly. Natural.' She decides to use white, green and yellow in her logo as they are colours that are associated with nature.

While looking at her competitors, Sally realises a lot of them use natural items such as roses or lavender in their photographs. She decides to use items related to each scent in her photographs. She tried using a large plinth but it didn't look appealing so Sally made her own version of a light box with a smaller plinth. She takes photographs on top of her tumble dryer as there is good lighting in that area of her house.

Sally decides to use a high-end cardboard tube with her logo stuck onto the side. She will later look at pre-made tubes once she is more established. She decides to add a free candle melt in each order, of the latest fragrance Sally is working on. Sally is also working on a discount code for that fragrance. She uses shredded paper so that she becomes eco-friendlier.

Chapter Four-Sally

Sally feels she could sell her candles on several platforms as her product is niche, but also appealing to people who are not that interested in eco-friendly products.

Her local town hall holds a craft market on every final Saturday of the month, so Sally decides to sign up and attend the market. She decides to skip Etsy and set up a website instead.

As Sally is fairly tech savvy, she decides to set up a website with a separate payment system (PayPal). She also opted to get a card reader from PayPal for her craft fair events.

Chapter Five-Sally

As Sally is using a website, she knows she needs to spend time perfecting her SEO. Sally will make sure that her headings and subtitles all contain keywords and phrases, while making sure these words don't look out of place. She knows she'll need to set time aside regularly to check her keywords are still relevant to her products.

Sally decides to use Facebook and Instagram. She is going to invest time on good images and well written posts.

She writes an example of a post she might use along with a photograph of a candle:

- *Sally Jones. Luxury. Eco-friendly. Natural*
- *Luxury Eco-Friendly Candles Made with Natural Essential Oils.*
- *Sally Jones- Luxury Candles specialise in providing luxury candles made with essential oils. To be as green as we can, all our packaging is also recyclable.*

Sally decides to use logs and natural products to display

her items. She knows that she is appealing to eco-friendly people. She will use recyclable card to display her information as well as recyclable packaging such as starch pellets and cardboard boxes.

She decides to do a competition but also focuses her blog on free information about candle making and blending scents. She also wants to blog about eco-friendly topics.

Sally uses lots of sensory words to describe the smell of her products. Words such as woody, deep, aromatic and floral. She adds her own tale of wanting to produce natural luxury products and how she decided to make them.

Chapter Six- Sally

Sally can't make all her candles to order but she can make some. She makes several of each scent and packs them ready. As they can take several days to cure, she wants to have a few ready to go that are individually packaged.

She decides to write all the orders she receives into a notebook which she will transfer at a later date to her Excel spreadsheet.

Sally will keep everything in a notebook and will write up at the end of the month into Excel. This will then be printed off and filed in a folder. She likes the idea of a folder to keep everything in as Sally tends to lose things. She will investigate what expenses she can claim to reduce her tax.

She has written her terms and conditions. She will accept cancellations as most of her candles are not made to order. She has checked on the Royal Mail website to see how long it would take for her candles to be delivered and has displayed this on her website. As her candles are not made to order, she will accept returns.

As she will mostly sell online, Sally will go for online focussed businesses accounts. She doesn't mind regularly moving accounts to save money.

Sally decides to keep a few draft replies for common issues she has via email. She looks at her polices to make sure they are easy to read and gets a few family members to double check them for her.

As Sally does sells in person and online, she decides to do two reports. She will use the same layout for both. Sally decides to monitor quarterly as her business can be seasonal. She likes the idea of breaking down her goals into smaller parts.

Sally knows she could possibly sell to both smaller and bigger stores if she adjusted her packaging to suit each store. She has a friend who also likes making candles who she could employ once in a while to help make the larger orders.

Chapter Seven-Sally

As Sally intends to start small, she is going to register as self-employed. She wants to scale up her business slowly over the next few years as her children get older and so will inquire about registering as a company at a later date.

While sally doesn't see herself setting up a company yet, she is going to try and keep good records in preparation should she decide to go down this route.

Being SE, Sally is finding it less scary than setting up a company. If she can make enough money, Sally will employ someone to help her make her candles even if it is only occasionally.

Sally is going to look at specific insurances for her candles. Candles can cause fires and she could not risk being personally sued as she could lose her home. She used several comparison sites to find a good deal that would suit her.

Sally knows she must follow CLP. She is unsure if her workspace counts for business rates so she will get in touch with her local council.

If Sally goes down the company route, she will look at trademarking her name to protect her business.

After completing a Self-Assessment form, Sally realises she needs to research better ways of keeping her customers data safe. She might investigate backing up the data. She uses a password protected hard drive to be safe, but she will check if that is acceptable under GDPR rules.

45

Rebecca

Rebecca lives with her partner and has one daughter. She is unsure about what she would like to make and sell but enjoys crafts such as sewing and jewellery making. She and her partner can just about afford to live on one salary but Rebecca would like to earn her own money too-ideally £500.

Chapter One-Rebecca

Rebecca would like more money and to find a new challenge. She has always liked crafts and thinks she could make a business out of it.

Rebecca hasn't thought of an idea yet but thinks that she is willing to put up with the cons such as working in the evening or the paperwork. The pros of being able to spend the days with her daughter and having enough for a holiday appeal to her.

After Rebecca and her partner sit down, they see they can save £50 on energy bills a month as well as both of them delaying upgrading their phones (£15 each). Long term, they agree to sell Rebecca's large car and get a smaller run around to cut insurance and petrol costs (£45).

As Rebecca hasn't got a formalised idea yet, she looks over what it would cost if she made and sold twenty of her handmade baby blankets. Her machine still works but it needs regular servicing, so she has built that into her costs.

- Cotton £40
- Fabric £140
- Waddling £180
- Trim £50
- Service machine £35
- Packaging £40
- Total: £485

Costs can be lowered depending on where Rebecca buys from and the quality of the materials. Rebecca also wants to sell on Etsy but have her own website too. The hosting and domain costs would be £20 per month.

Rebecca thinks she might need to get a small grant or loan. She draws up the pros and cons of several options and decides to try The Prince's Trust. She will need to write a business plan.

She thinks she is likely to overspend and under price her products. She has decided she needs to remember she is making to sell not to keep her products, so needs to keep costs low and cut back on unnecessary extras.

Rebecca is already part of several hobby sewing groups on Facebook but joins a niche group for people who sew and sell on Etsy. Rebecca lives near to a regional business support centre so decides to attend an event to get some ideas for her business. She comes away with some helpful literature on how to set up a business and where to get extra support.

Chapter Two - Rebecca

During the exercise, Rebecca found several ideas that she might consider. After narrowing down ideas, she decides to make reusable beauty products such as face pads or sanitary products. She owns some herself but finds the patterns unattractive and wants to make them more 'feminine'.

Rebecca decides Facebook groups are a good place to ask for advice and conduct research. She asks the members of her sewing group what annoys them the most about hand-sewn items, but specifically hand-sewn beauty products. She gets a lot of responses so narrows it down to just the sanitary products. She also conducts research on Etsy and Google. After looking at reviews, the main issues seem to be:

- Lack of absorbency
- Design
- Cost

Rebecca finds products with excellent reviews to build a picture of what her ideal customer would look like. Her ideal customer would be 18-40 years old, female, want to save money and the planet but also is interested in well-designed products.

Her USP's are:

- Highly absorbent
- Feminine design
- Low/affordable cost
- *Highly absorbent with feminine designs at affordable prices.*

Rebecca has added notes on whether she needs specialised licenses (she doesn't think she does but will check). She has filled in a few sections of her business plan but will fill in the rest as she goes on. If she thinks of an idea for a section of the plan she hasn't yet reached, she writes it on a sticky note and places it next to the corresponding area in the plan.

She decides to rely on bigger chains for most of her stock. She found a good variety on eBay of trimmings and fabric.

Rebecca is using Option Two as she is unsure how much she could sell her products for, so she wants to start selling at a lower price to test the market. She will start with £5 profit per pack. She can make five packs an hour so her hourly rate is £25.

She decides to use her USP's and her favourite colour for her name: Pink Eco Cloths.

Chapter Three- Rebecca

Rebecca starts making the pads and she would like to focus on eco-friendly materials to make environmentally friendly products. As her name has pink in it, she decides to use shades of pink for her logo.

She buys a small light box. Lots of her competitors use hardly any props so Rebecca buys cardboard stands to lean her products on. This looks better than just laying them flat.

Rebecca decides to go for a cost-effective brown paper mail bag but wrap items in recycled tissue paper which is sealed with her logo as a sticker. After working out her costs, she knows packing materials will cost her 50p per order. When Rebecca can afford to buy in bulk, she knows her costs will also go down.

Chapter Four- Rebecca

Although Rebecca feels she could dedicate time to set up her own website, she is more confident in using a ready-made platform such as Etsy for the time being.

Her county has several fairs and markets over the next few months. Rebecca is going to enquire about those although she feels she will make more money on her online shop. She likes the idea of gaining experience with customers.

Rebecca is keen to look at all solutions to payment systems for her in person payments. She likes the look of Square and will conduct more research. As she is mostly selling with Etsy, she doesn't need to consider extra payment methods (as Etsy handle all of this), although she will look at a business bank account.

Chapter Five- Rebecca

Although selling through Etsy, SEO can still be relevant, so Rebecca has searched Etsy for words (menstrual pad, cloth pad etc) along with making sure her descriptions in Etsy contain her keywords such as 'Eco/Environmentally friendly'.

Rebecca has decided to use Instagram and Pinterest for her social media promotions. She is going to add topics to her website that encourage people to move towards eco-friendly living. She can also share this on her social media accounts.

She knows that her ideal social media customer would be:

- 18 +
- Like shopping, eco-friendly living, nature and handmade goods.

- Female
- Located around the world
- Use social media regularly and like posts that can be shared.ie. funny/motivational.

Rebecca is worried that her items are not good enough to sell. She feels doing a few fairs and talking with customers would make her feel more confident.

She decides to use boxes and natural goods like flowers as props for her products.

Rebecca decides to run a competition and give free pouches away with all of her orders. She always has spare fabric, so it adds to the 'eco-friendly image' to reduce waste.

She knows her product faces the problem of a lot of plastic waste. She decides to use this as a key selling tactic in that she is actively trying to reduce waste in her business. She also focuses on the femininity of her range to appeal to women who value this in their products.

Rebecca adds a short tale about how she couldn't find products like hers when looking so she decided to make them herself.

Chapter Six-Rebecca

Rebecca will initially start with a small stash of fabric samples so she can pre-make all of her designs. As they become popular, she will buy more stock of the most popular designs and less of her least popular designs. Rebecca can then make items ready to ship which will reduce her processing time and make her more appealing to customers.

She decides to write her orders and expenses into an

app her on her phone. She then types these onto a spreadsheet at the end of the month.

Rebecca will keep a computer-based system for tax. She will keep the spreadsheet and add to it weekly. She will look into whether she can claim for her stationary in her expenses.

She decides not to accept cancellations as she will be initially making items to order. She will only accept returns if damaged or unused.

As Rebecca will be doing mixed sales (both online and in-person), she needs an account that allows both types of sales. She struggles to find a bank account that caters equally to both, so decides the she will focus on a mostly online based account. So she opts for an online business account deal.

Rebecca decides to make sure she has a return form ready should someone want to return under EU rules. She decides to keep the same rules for everyone in regard to polices.

Rebecca monitors her business monthly as it isn't seasonal. Rebecca decides to do small tasks each week that add to a larger goal every quarter.

Rebecca feels smaller shops would be a better fit for her. Rebecca thinks she'd struggle to sell to larger shops without having to comprise on her eco-friendly message. She also doesn't think she'd make enough profit if she sold in bulk quantities.

Chapter Seven- Rebecca

Rebecca hasn't got a huge desire to be a large company. She wants to start small and get a good work/life balance. She feels overwhelmed at all of the company paperwork she'd have to do.

She finds setting up as self-employed very easy.

Rebecca will keep simple records and enquire about filling out tax forms with the Tax Office to see if they have advice.

Rebecca decides to get basic insurance for her business. She is more worried about damage to her stock and equipment than her products hurting someone else as this is unlikely.

The only regulation Rebecca can find is about labelling fabric (EU 1007/2011) but she isn't sure if it is relevant. She is going to email her local Trading Standards to double check.

Rebecca is not going to look at a trademark as she doesn't see her business having issues with wanting to expand and needing one.

She needs to check her website and data processing methods on the data processing Self-Assessment form to make sure she is complying will all the GDPR regulations.

PART IX

Appendix

46

Facebook Groups to Join

<u>Candles</u>

- Taking the Wick for Candle Makers
- DIY Candle Making: Beginner to Advanced
- Candle Making by Candle Makers
- Candle Makers Resource Group
- Homemade Candle Creations
- Beginner Beeswax Candle Making
- Candle and Craft

<u>Sewing</u>

- I Love Sewing
- Sewing Crafts and Chat UK
- Sewing for Babies and Children
- Beginner Sewing

Knitting

- Knitting and Crochet Makers
- Addiction to Knitting
- Knitting and Crochet Pattern Designer Team
- Knitting Café

Jewellery

- Jewellery Makers United
- Jewellery Makers Treasure Trove
- Jewellery Making Ideas
- DIY Jewellery Making
- ACJ Community
- Jewellery Making Addicts Anonymous

Cakes

- Cake Decorating Support Group
- Cake Decorating and Advice
- Cake Decorating Tutorials

Soap Making and Beauty

- Soap Recipes World
- Soap Making for Beginners Worldwide
- Soap Making
- Soap Making 101
- Organic and Homemade Beauty Recipes

- Homemade Beauty Products

Generic support

- Making Mumpreneurs Club
- GDPR For Online Entrepreneurs
- The Unique Mumpreneur Community
- 3-day Workweek: Full-Time Income. Part Time Hours
- Crafts on a Budget Official
- Creative Superheroes
- Creative Hive VIP

47

Four Ways to Organise Your Business with OneNote

- Have separate notebooks set up to accept receipts based on either a time period (i.e. weekly or monthly) or sorted on the basis of what they are for (i.e. Stock or fair fees). Within these notebooks you can add individual sections (which act like pages) where you can deposit each receipt. I would recommend one receipt per section as well as getting into a habit of detailed labelling to make for easy searching.
- Set up separate notebooks for each new project to keep your workspace more organised. If you make several different types of product, then having a separate note section for each means you can drop your new ideas in the relevant area.
- Use notebooks to keep information. Keep all information about each item you make in one notebook. If you made candles, you'd make a section per new type of candle. In this section you would include an image, a description, weight, ingredients and process of making. This

can be particularly helpful if you sell in person as you can bring up the information in front of a customer for them to see it too on your tablet or phone.

- A notebook for Short and Long-Term Goals. In my notebook, I have broken down all my larger goals into smaller tasks in order to make the goal seem less intimidating. As you can add tick boxes in OneNote, it is satisfying being able to tick off a task as you complete it.

48

Five Ways to Save Money in Your Business

1. Limit Your Stock: Only buy what you know you will soon run out of and avoid buying extra products on sale under the guise you are actually saving yourself money. Unless the item is rarely reduced or a large, planned for purchase then don't be tempted. If something should go wrong with your business, you don't want to be stuck with hundreds of pounds worth of stock that you would struggle to shift.

2. Limit How Much Material You Need for Each Project: Work out what are the bare minimums you need to make your item and stick to those materials. Unless the extra accessories you are adding on to the item will warrant a higher sale price, find a way to remove them from your process.

3. Reduce Quality Level in Your Stock: If you sell items that have a large price tag, then this model will not work. Your customers would feel cheated and that is not a feeling you want your customers to think. Check if you are buying

expensive materials that materials as a selling point, make sure you emphasise this in your description of the product.

4. Cut Your Postage Costs: Go to your local Post Office and ask what sort of packages they have for small businesses. Some services will even come and pick up the packages from you to save you going to the Post Office yourself. Also see if you could reduce the cost of your packaging materials. Something as simple as choosing a smaller box to post your items in can save you not only money on the cost of the packing materials but it can also reduce how much postage you pay.

5. Routinely Change Your Suppliers: Some suppliers will offer discounts for bulk orders which could be an option to investigate once you are more established. Built it in to your calendar to set aside a few hours once a quarter to see if you could find a better deal for your business.

49

Weekly Business Tasks Checklist

Banking Tasks

- Regular payments
- Fraudulent spending
- Enough cash flow

Set Tasks or Goals for the Week

- List goals and tasks
- Break down large tasks/goals into smaller bits

Social Media Tasks

- Check statistics
- Reply to messages
- Engage in comments
- Run giveaways

- Design new adverts/engagement posts
- Schedule posts you want and when you want to post them

Research Tasks

- Current trends
- Emerging trends
- What is your competition doing?

Recording Tasks

- Tax spreadsheet
- Statistics
- Receipts/costs
- Postage
- Stock check- do you need to buy anything this week

Email Tasks

- Send emails
- Respond to emails
- Clear inbox

Product Tasks

- Take photos of new products/refresh old photographs
- Update descriptions
- Pack and ship items
- Design new products
- Make individual and wholesale orders

Branding Board

You can find creative ways of displaying your Branding Board on places such as Pinterest. You can print a template so that you can cut and stick your ideas onto the page. For the more technologically savvy, you could make a board yourself using programmes such as InDesign or Photoshop. Alternatively, set up either a paper or digital notebook page and drop ideas into it.

You will want to include the following topics on your Branding Board:

Back story

- why do you want to make/sell your items?

Colour palette

- Colour 1
- Colour 2

- Colour 3
- Colour 4
- Colour 5

Typography

- Font 1
- Font 2
- Font 3

Tagline

- What is your tagline?

Logo

- What does your logo look like?

NOTES

NOTES